National Parks for Life ... National Parks for everyone. Blencathra in the Lake District National Park. Photo: Ian Brodie

In 1996 we asked a selection of people the question: Why are National Parks important to look after for this and future generations?

"Our National Parks are areas of exceptional value each with special qualities of national and international importance, and I believe they are in a strong position to influence the way in which we care for our countryside and to be models for the sustainable management of the wider countryside". John Gummer MP, Environment Secretary

"In a world with too few opportunities for quiet contemplation, refreshment of mind and spirit and reverence for the beauty of creation, it is our duty to look after the National Parks with the utmost care and respect". Dr George Carey, Archbishop of Canterbury

"National Parks are the first places we seek when we need to refresh spirits eroded by the pressure of modern life. We must ensure that those who follow us can gain the highest values of re-creation". Ian Brodie, Friends of the Lake District

"I want to make sure that our children have the same opportunity to enjoy National Parks as all those who have enjoyed and admired the Parks since they were set up almost fifty years ago". Tony Blair MP, Leader of the Labour Party

"The National Park, with its stunning landscapes and rich diversity of wildlife and cultural heritage, is my shop window for the wider environmental debate". Tim Braund, Exmoor National Park area ranger

"We are but stewards of the land, our duty is to pass it on in good heart and enhance its beauty. We must conserve it, not just preserve it". Christopher Tomson, Farm Manager, Broomhead Estate, Peak National Park

"We haven't much time left to reconcile economic development and environmental care and protection and I would like to see National Parks at the cutting edge of finding answers: I would hate us to say to future generations, `well we knew about the problems, but lacked the courage to try the solutions'." Frances Rowe, Northumberland National Park Authority chairman

"So that all generations may enjoy and understand them and, from that basis, apply the principles of sustainable management everywhere". The Earl of Cranbrook, English Nature chairman

"One of the fundamental principles of running a successful water business is the recognition that we must act with responsibility to protect and enhance sensitive environments, such as our National Parks, for the community which we serve and for future generations". Mike Crabtree, Head of Conservation, Access and Recreation, North West Water

"Future generations deserve the chance to enjoy and understand our finest living landscapes, their ecology and their cultural heritage". Christopher Harrison, Peak National Park Officer

"As the drab tide of urbanisation floods unchecked over the green face of our land, National Parks may ultimately prove to be the only places where walkers may still stretch their legs and breath country air". Ken Willson, Ramblers' Association, West Riding Area

"In this overcrowded island, half the size of France but with the same size population, and where most of us live in cities, we all need periodically the refreshment of visiting a green, unchanging countryside; in our National Parks we hope this heritage will be protected now and for many generations to come". Joan Pye, a Friend of National Parks

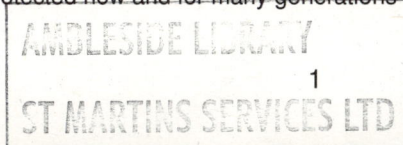

The Council for National Parks (CNP) is the charity which promotes the conservation, quiet enjoyment and understanding of the National Parks of England and Wales.

This report has been prepared as part of a major CNP project, supported by the Dennis Curry Charitable Trust, on how to protect and use National Parks in an environmentally sustainable way. It contains messages for Government and other public bodies, National Park Authorities, companies, environmental organisations and consumers. A report specifically for companies, "Not Ours, But Ours to Look After", is also available from the Council for National Parks, 246 Lavender Hill London SW11 1LJ.

During the course of the project the Council for National Parks has consulted widely and has worked closely with the Corporate Forum for National Parks. This group of leading companies recognises the unique value of National Parks for conservation and recreation, and agrees to uphold National Park values in the development and application of environmental policies.

This report was researched and written by Vicki Elcoate, the Council for National Parks' Director of Projects.

Hilary Welch was the design consultant. The photographs by Chris Swan were commissioned thanks to a generous donation from Miss Joan Pye. Simon Gilbert of Artewisdom (London) produced the "virtual reality" computer landscapes.

Acknowledgements

The Council for National Parks would particularly like to thank the following for their help in the preparation of this report: Peter Abbott (Peak National Park); Ian Brodie (Friends of the Lake District); Jim Bull (CNP); the Earl of Cranbrook (English Nature); Keith Davies (Countryside Council for Wales); Michelle Greenwald (BTCV); Angus Lunn (CNP); Rick Minter (Countryside Commission); Ann MacEwen (planning consultant and author); Amanda Nobbs (CNP); Adrian Phillips (IUCN); Matt Phillips (Friends of the Earth); Tim O'Riordan (University of East Anglia); Siân Phipps (CPRE); Colin Speakman (Yorkshire Dales Society); Andy Wilson (Northumberland National Park).

Thanks also to National Park Authority ecologists and minerals planners for help with data included in this report. Participants in a land management seminar are acknowledged in that section.

Summary

National Parks for Life

The vision of National Parks in 2040:

Beautiful landscapes where:

- water, soil and air are pure
- natural landforms are preserved
- wildlife flourishes
- a range of distinctive cultures is expressed in the built heritage and the everyday lives of Park residents
- livelihoods derive from activities that the environment can sustain

- erosion of the special qualities would not be contemplated unless society could find no other possible solution
- everyone can find a source of spiritual renewal and opportunities for quiet enjoyment
- we can all gain a greater understanding of the whole environment and of National Park values

---

National Parks are:

- critical to achieving national and international sustainable development objectives;
- areas where the protection of integrity is of paramount importance;
- critical to species', including human, survival in the face of current predictions on climate change;

- on such a large scale that there is enormous potential for the enhancement of natural beauty, biodiversity and cultural heritage;
- to be regarded as models for the whole countryside and pinnacles of environmental achievement, not islands of sustainability.

Their sustainability is threatened by:

- demand for energy (producing climate change and acidification);
- intensification and diversification of agriculture;
- increasing demand for aggregates;
- road transport;

- development, including associated activities like changes in recreational activity;
- degradation of water quality;
- demand for water.

The report contains many messages for different interest groups which would protect National Parks from these unsustainable trends. It also identifies opportunities for sustainable development which can be seized now. It has three key messages for Government:

- **All Government departments should demonstrate clearly how they are implementing their duty in the 1995 Environment Act to have regard to the Park purposes. This would achieve better protection for National Parks and enable sustainable development to be progressed across a significant area of countryside;**

- **Maintaining an adequate level of funding to National Park Authorities, as the National Parks Review Panel recommended is a cost effective way of delivering sustainable development. The level of funding announced at the end of 1996 is a first step in this direction;**

- **The designation of new National Parks, notably the New Forest and South Downs which meet the criteria for designation, is a pressing need in the light of sustainability objectives on biodiversity, tourism and the conservation of lowland landscapes.**

Contents

Section 1: This Common Inheritance: where National Parks fit in

"The future is on our side to no small degree, if we can hold the fort for another generation" (Foreword by G. M. Trevelyan, CPRE 1932)

National Parks are entering a new era and this report aims to inspire those who will be setting a new agenda for them. The original National Parks' legislation was nearly fifty years ago. This report aims to build on the National Park measures in the 1995 Environment Act to set an agenda that will equip the Parks for the next fifty years. This report links National Parks into the debates on sustainable development and sustainability. It looks at what we must do today in relation to National Parks to ensure that the ability of future generations to meet their own needs is not compromised. This is a matter both of the means of survival and a good quality of life.

In the 1949 National Parks and Access to the Countryside Act the National Park purposes were stated as: preserving and enhancing the natural beauty of the areas and promoting their enjoyment by the public.

The 1995 Environment Act, following the recommendations of the National Parks Review Panel (Edwards 1991), reflected more fully how the original purposes have always been interpreted: conserving and enhancing the natural beauty, wildlife and cultural heritage of the areas and promoting opportunities for the understanding and enjoyment of their special qualities by the public.

The new purposes harmonise with the objectives of sustainability, by bringing in the enhancement of biodiversity and by adding the human dimension in relation to beautiful landscapes.

What is a National Park?

After the Second World War there was public support for a system of National Parks as part of a "better world" "for those who had endured so much" (Sir Norman Birkett QC 1945).

The idea was inspired by the wilderness, state-owned National Parks in the United States and by the romantic poet William Wordsworth who conceived of the Lake District as "a sort of national property" (1810). The National Parks of England and Wales designated under the 1949 National Parks and Access to the Countryside Act, however, have a mixed system of land ownership and a legacy of human influence on the landscape going back 5,000 years.

In the 1950s the first ten Parks were designated: the Peak District; the Lake District; Snowdonia; Dartmoor; Pembrokeshire Coast; North York Moors; Yorkshire Dales; Exmoor; Northumberland; the Brecon Beacons.

The National Parks of England and Wales (Scotland has none) are all designated for the conservation and enhancement of the natural beauty of the landscape, the wildlife and cultural heritage and for the promotion of opportunities for understanding and enjoyment. The Broads, designated more recently, has a third purpose relating to the traditional rights of navigation on its waterways.

Each is run by a National Park Authority, which has a majority of local authority members and a minority appointed by the Secretary of State. Most of the funding comes directly from central government. The 1995 Environment Act made them free-standing bodies within local government. The National Parks Review Panel said the advantage was to give them "clarity of vision and self-confidence" and "would allow the National Park Authority to set its own agenda and pursue it resolutely" (Edwards 1991). All National Park Authorities are responsible for drawing up a management plan and development plans and for deciding planning applications within that context.

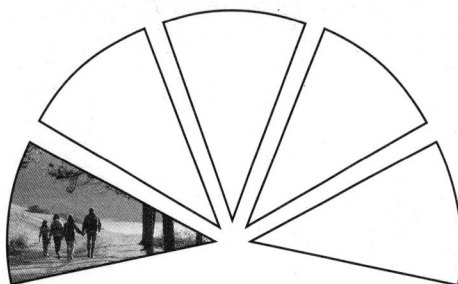

Sustainable Development and Sustainability

The aim of sustainable development was defined by the Brundtland Commission (World Commission on Environment and Development 1987) as "to meet the needs of present generations without compromising the ability of future generations to meet their own needs". Of course, much depends on the definition of "needs". It was a big turning point as it introduced the idea of the environment into theories about economic development. The idea implies the integration of environmental and social objectives into economic decision making.

Brundtland said sustainable development included the central ideas of: equity amongst current generations alive on earth; equity between people alive now and in the future; protection of natural systems; natural capital stock; limits to economic growth; global inter-dependency; and the need to merge environment and economics in decision-making.

The Government sees it as the combination of: achieving economic development to secure a higher standard of living now and for future generations whilst protecting and enhancing the environment (UK Government 1994).

Development should not be confused with growth, although politicians often do. "Although there are limits to growth, there are no limits to development" (Meadows et al 1992). "When something grows it gets quantitatively bigger; when it develops it gets qualitatively better, or at least different. Quantitative growth and qualitative improvement follow different laws. Our planet develops over time without growing. Our economy, a subsystem of the finite and non-growing earth, must eventually adapt to a similar pattern of development (Goodland et al 1991, Meadows et al cit.)."

The concept of sustainability removes the potential for confusion about growth and recognises that where a balance is not possible the environment takes precedence. Sustainability is when policies are environment-led and growth is not an objective. It implies limits on activity, development and change. It unties the knot between development and economic growth, providing opportunities for new ways of doing things.

Critical natural capital is central to the discussion of limits. Pearce (1993) defined the concept of "critical natural capital" as that which is critical to survival or well-being. This report argues that National Parks constitute critical natural capital vital both to survival and well-being. It proposes that the limits to or path of development must be made clear and that opportunities should be grasped to take full advantage of the potential of the Parks to contribute to quality of life and well-being.

The 1995 Act brings a wider range of players to the National Park table, giving greater scope for partnerships. It gives public bodies, including private companies defined as "statutory undertakers", a duty to have regard to the National Park purposes in their activities affecting the Parks. The circular (12/96) accompanying the National Park clauses in the Act also asks National Park Authorities to involve a wider cross section of interest groups, including companies, to share in a vision of more sustainable National Park futures, in the non-statutory National Park Plans.

The Act gives National Park Authorities, in pursuing their purposes, a duty to foster the socio-economic well-being of local communities – a duty that should be consistent with the aims of sustainable development. This is discussed further in Section 4.

The Act also brings, as of right, parish council members onto National Park Authorities, enabling Park communities to focus more clearly on the National Park purposes.

It also puts the Sandford principle into legislation, by stating that when the two purposes conflict every effort must be made to achieve a reconciliation. Where an irreconcilable conflict exists, the conservation purpose takes precedence.

National Parks are places where the environment leads policies and the 1995 Environment Act provides some of the ingredients for putting into practice sustainability – a way of living that does not degrade and should enhance the environment.

The test for major development in National Parks, in Planning Policy Guidance Note 7 and Planning Guidance (Wales) includes many ideas

A brighter future?

Summary

National Park Authorities have years of experience in encouraging environmentally-friendly land management. This means working to achieve a balance of the needs of conservation and public recreation whilst working with local communities and others with an interest in the Park. The 1995 legislation and accompanying guidance create a new climate for enabling that expertise to be broadened to include other issues: tackling pollution by working with private companies or demand for water and energy by working with consumers, for instance.

Below are some examples of where National Park Authorities have promoted more sustainable land management with great benefits to National Parks and their communities.

Farm schemes

All the National Parks now have farm schemes which include advice on landscape and wildlife conservation as well as direct agricultural economic advice and top-up grants for conservation work. One of the most comprehensive schemes, set up in 1990 in the North York Moors National Park, has enjoyed a good level of take up in the dales where it operates and has had demonstrable conservation successes. These schemes are discussed in more detail later in the report.

Native woods

Managing woodlands in National Parks is an important job for National Park Authorities. The Peak National Park has won a series of awards for its woodland management and has a rolling programme for acquiring small woods, restoring them and then re-selling them with conditions. The Northumberland National Park has used lottery money to purchase ancient woodland and put it into sustainable management.

The Association of National Park Authorities and the Forestry Authority have an agreement to work together to increase native woodlands in National Parks. Some bold targets have been set to implement this. The Yorkshire Dales National Park has a target to create 2,000 hectares of new broad-leaved woodland over the next 25 years: double the present extent. Some National Park Societies, like the Friends of the Lake District, are also creating areas of native woodland.

Rare habitats

The Broads Authority spends more than 50% of its budget on conservation, managing a rare wetland habitat that includes reedbeds – a habitat that has declined by 40 per cent since 1945. Reedbeds need to be managed or they quickly deteriorate. The Broads Authority is encouraging reedbed management, including commercial production – cutting the reeds for thatching. At present the UK imports reeds so extension and management of the reedbeds may become self-funding through sale of the product. The reedbeds support a unique range of wildlife, most notably the swallow-tail butterfly and the bittern, a rare member of the heron family.

Reed cutting in the Broads. Photo: Chris Swan

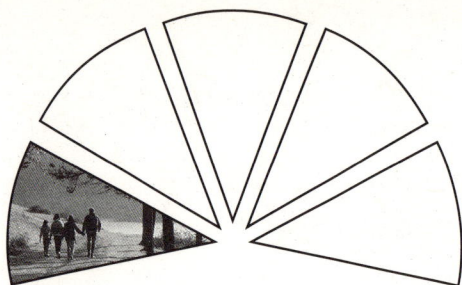

central to sustainable development. Major development in the Parks should not take place save in exceptional circumstances and should be subject to a rigorous examination. It should be assessed against strict criteria including whether there is a national need and whether that need can be met in an alternative way. Sustainable development questions the need for physical development which takes up yet more land and uses more natural resources and may cause pollution. It makes us consider how best society's needs can be met: for example we should ask "does that road really need to be built or is there another solution to our transport problems"? That approach is now well enshrined in the Government's policies for the Parks.

Greenprints for the countryside

Lessons learnt in National Parks often have much wider application, including in urban areas. They are part of the whole countryside as well as being beacons for it: the MacEwens (1987) called them "greenprints for the countryside."

The MacEwens, however, saw the Parks as prototypes, not perfected models, which begs the question: are today's National Parks able to act as greenprints as the Government intends?

The Government's 1990 White Paper, This Common Inheritance, stated: "Our National Parks are the jewels in the countryside's crown ... they are important in themselves and set standards for the countryside as a whole". The National Parks Review Panel looked at these issues in detail (Edwards 1991). It recognised that the concept of sustainable use was "in line with the objectives of the National Parks. The Parks could therefore serve as one demonstration of, or test bed for, the nation's commitment to sustainable use". Some of the

achievements of Park Authorities on sustainable land management are outlined in the case-study, "A Brighter Future?".

The Rural White Paper (Department of the Environment/MAFF 1995) introduced a strong theme of sustainable development into rural policy. On designated areas, including National Parks, it said: "While it is important not to weaken protection of designated areas, the approaches pioneered in them can now be applied throughout our countryside".

Circular 12/96 says: "National Parks are in a strong position to influence the way we care for our countryside, to be models for the sustainable management of the wider countryside, and to help further general understanding and appreciation of the means by which development and conservation can be better balanced". This gives National Parks a central role not only in practising sustainable development but also in demonstrating their achievements to a much wider audience.

But, on many fronts, Government policy over many years has failed National Parks because, as Section 3 finds, there is still evidence of deteriorating environmental quality (Edwards 1991). As the MacEwens (1987) pointed out, National Parks can only be greenprints if they are supported by Government policy, including economic policy, which would give them adequate resources and better protection from damaging activities and trends like minerals extraction, military training, road building, water abstraction, nuclear power, intensive farming and forestry.

In this report's vision of a sustainable future, National Parks should be not only greenprints for the countryside but also "pinnacles" or "beacons", demonstrating what can be achieved, rather than "islands" of sustainability.

National Parks and their place in the world

The World Conservation Union (IUCN) has looked at the contribution to sustainable development of Protected Areas (into which international category the English and Welsh National Parks fall). It has called for the "integration of protected areas with national planning for sustainable development, with sustainable development at the local level, with planning of the use of land and sea, and with control of pollution" (IUCN 1994).

An initiative to take forward Chapter 13 of Agenda 21 (United Nations 1992), the comprehensive programme for sustainable development which was produced by the United Nations 1990 conference on Environment and Development (the Earth Summit), provides another opportunity for placing National Parks in a global context. The inclusion of this Chapter gives sustainable mountain development a global priority rating comparable to tropical rainforest depletion, desertification, ozone depletion and climate change.

Chapter 13 focuses on "managing fragile ecosystems: sustainable mountain development". Most of the National Parks of England and Wales represent the mountain ecosystems which Chapter 13 addresses. Although they do not fall into the category of mountains by virtue of altitude – they would simply be called uplands – their climate, soil, ecosystems and scale and role in the surrounding landscape are that of mountains. Their relationship with lowland areas – the supply of natural resources outwards and the flow of visitors inwards – equates with mountainous areas in other countries.

Chapter 13 recognises the importance of mountain areas as a source for water, energy and biological diversity, as well as a source of key resources such as minerals, forest and agricultural products and of recreation. "As a major ecosystem representing the complex and interrelated ecology of our planet, mountain environments are essential to the survival of the global ecosystem" (op. cit.). It particularly recognises the role of mountain communities in conserving mountain ecosystems and the urgent need to address their socio-economic difficulties.

A process of inter-governmental consultation is drawing up a programme of action on sustainable mountain development, a process to which CNP is committed.

Delegates from twenty European countries and the European Commission have agreed recommendations (see next page) which will have implications for British Government policy, in particular how policies for National Parks are integrated across all areas of policy. Case-study 1.3 on two National Park mountain areas raises some important issues.

Criticality

The Government's Sustainable Development Strategy (1994) states that "within the various types of designated area, those of international importance could be deemed closest to being inviolable natural capital". Into that category clearly fall "sites protected in order to meet international obligations" (for instance, Special Areas for Conservation and Ramsar sites).

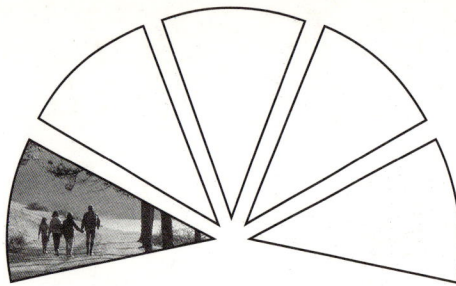

Recommendations of European governments and the European Commission on sustainable mountain development, as part of the process for taking forward the Rio "Earth Summit" on sustainable development

Promote sustainable mountain programmes

Develop environmentally sustainable mountain action plans and programmes demonstrating the long-term benefit of compatible multi-purpose land management

Promote sustainable mountain agriculture and forestry

Link environmental quality, conservation and recreational value to the allocation of funding

Assess the impacts of existing national and European policies with respect to environmental and societal benefit, and give greater priority to positive incentives for land management instead of only production

Promote sustainable transport and energy policies

Adjust the modal split [eg road/rail] in order to reduce road traffic in accordance with the principles of sustainable development through appropriate economic, infrastructural and technical measures and incentives

Reconsider investment in infrastructure which is not environmentally sustainable

Stimulate energy savings and efficient energy use

Promote the role of ecologically sensitive and protected areas in sustainable mountain strategies

Promote areas which are designated in recognition of their natural heritage for testing and demonstrating environmentally sustainable sound practices

As far as possible, the remaining mountain ecosystems with minimum human impacts should be protected for the benefit of present and future generations

Develop criteria, indicators and information systems

Develop criteria for evaluating sustainable mountain development policies

Publicise widely significant case studies of success and failure, with respect to sustainable mountain development, in the European mountains

Develop appropriate instruments for sustainable mountain development

Develop appropriate legal, economic, financial and planning instruments to foster sustainable mountain development

Promote international co-operation for sustainable mountain development

Promote international co-operation at all levels, and especially through networks of demonstration projects, protected areas, research centres etc., across the mountains of Europe

An integrated cross-sectoral approach, as well as more sustainable sectoral policies, especially for agriculture, forestry, transport, tourism and energy is required

(Source: European Inter-governmental Commission on Sustainable Mountain Development. IUCN, 1996)

The Government's Strategy has a heavy emphasis on sites designated for nature conservation. It goes on to state that "those of national importance must be protected, but may need to be traded against equally important economic objectives, in which case it may be necessary to look at the scope for designating compensatory resources".

This theme was echoed by the report of the House of Lords Select Committee on Sustainable Development (1995). It supported the differentiation between "vital, irreplaceable and non-substitutable elements in the environment" (Dr Susan Owens, evidence to the Committee) which involved "major life or planet threatening concerns" and "more modest or

local concerns which may be capable of negotiated trade-offs" (Committee findings).

The National Parks of England and Wales are vital, irreplaceable and non-substitutable elements in the environment. They are part of a critical network of protected areas across Europe, where the enhancement of biodiversity, landscape beauty and cultural heritage is paramount. The Government has yet to address the critical importance to sustainability objectives of the network of Protected Areas, of which our National Parks are a significant part.

Current thinking places fresh emphasis on the importance of conservation at the landscape level which was "until recently ... the poor relation of biodiversity" (Bridgewater 1996). The importance of the discipline of landscape ecology, which considers the development and dynamics of landscapes across space and time

is fundamental to the consideration of major issues, like climate change (discussed further in Section 3).

Bridgewater argues that natural ecosystems will be less able to withstand climate change because of the impact of land use and human activities. In the past it was possible to recover from dramatic climate change because species were able "to change their distribution boundaries, or migrate to refugia" (Stock 1992, Bridgewater cit.). Today those options have largely disappeared, often remaining only through the network of Protected Areas. Management for climate change is discussed later in this report. However the importance of National Parks in helping much wider areas adapt to climate change and in resisting "the extinction process we have already set in train by poor land use allocation and management" makes them critical to survival in the future.

Section Summary

National Parks are:

☀ critical to achieving national and international sustainable development objectives;

☀ areas where the protection of integrity is of paramount importance;

☀ essential to the provision of opportunities for recreation and enjoyment in ways that depend on and are in harmony with the special qualities of the Parks;

☀ on such a large scale that there is enormous potential for the enhancement of natural beauty, biodiversity and cultural heritage;

☀ critical to the survival of species, including humans, in the face of predictions on climate change;

☀ to be regarded as models for the whole countryside and pinnacles of environmental achievement, not islands of sustainability.

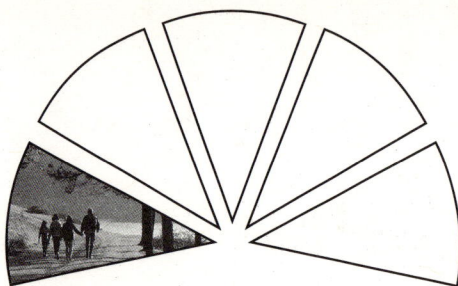

Just a local matter . . .

Summary

Although Government policy states that National Parks enjoy the "highest status of landscape protection" (Department of the Environment/Welsh Office 1992) the practice of Government departments is not always consistent with this. The recent changes in legislation, the national importance of the National Park designation and the policy context for minerals planning must bring about a change in the way Ministers regard major applications for damaging development in National Parks, when a case for a call-in has been made.

The Government has set out its policy considerations for minerals planning (DoE 1996) in Moving Towards Sustainable Development. This includes a specific policy "to protect areas of designated landscape or nature conservation value from development, other than in exceptional circumstances and where it has been demonstrated that development is in the public interest". Planning Policy Guidance Note 7 and Minerals Planning Policy Guidance Note 6 (for aggregates) apply this to National Parks specifically and make a rigorous examination of such applications essential (see page 38). These guidelines operate within a planning system where a presumption exists in favour of the development plan, so that any departure from the plan should be referred to the Secretary of State.

Some examples:

1994: 21 acre extension to Goddards Quarry in the Peak Park (involving a departure from the Structure Plan).

> Environment Minister: "Planning applications are ... in general only called-in if planning issues of much more than local importance are involved, and if those issues need to be decided by the Secretary of State rather than at local level ... He has, therefore decided not to call-in the planning application to extend Goddards Quarry for his own decision" (letter to CNP May 1994).

1995: Open cast slate quarrying at Rhosydd Quarry in the Snowdonia National Park (the applicants later changed the application voluntarily to exclude the part in the Park).

> Welsh Office: "In this case it was concluded that the proposed development does not involve planning issues which warrant taking the application out of local hands" (letter to CNP October 1995).

1995: major extension to Swinden Quarry in the Yorkshire Dales.

> Environment Minister: "examples of cases where call-in may be appropriate are those which could have wide effects beyond their immediate locality; those which give rise to substantial regional or national controversy; those which may conflict with national policy on important matters; and those where the interests of national security or a foreign government may be involved ... I take the view that in this case it is right to leave the decision to be taken by the planning authority" (letter to CNP June 1995).

1995: extension of vein mineral workings at Moss Rake East in the Peak Park (departure from the Structure plan).

> Environment Secretary: exactly the same words as in above letter (letter to CNP October 1995)

The above examples suggest that the action of Ministers conflicts with Government policy on National Parks.

National Parks are a national designation supported by national policy to protect their long term interests. Minerals developments in them have a serious impact on Park purposes. The Government's role in conflicts between different kinds of interests is to enable a strategic debate on the issues. The decision by the Secretary of State to call in an application to extend working at Spaunton Quarry in the North York Moors does recognise this role and provides an opportunity for the right kind of questions to be raised.

Major developments in National Parks are much more than local matters and Ministers should look more positively on requests for a call-in when serious doubts have been raised as to whether the development should be justified on the grounds of overriding national need.

Mountains: just a view, a brew and a loo?

Summary

The mountain environment is particularly valuable in England and Wales because there is so little of it. Mountainous areas in National Parks contain fragile ecosystems, support species at the edge of their ranges, sustain a way of life that is rapidly disappearing and provide opportunities for "back to nature" or "wilderness" enjoyment and experiences which are limited elsewhere. Without these qualities the mountainous areas of England and Wales will become just like anywhere else – supporting an entirely urban experience – only higher up. What should the future be?

Snowdon Summit

At 1085 metres, the Snowdon massif is one of the honeypot attractions in the Snowdonia National Park. Yet not only is it an inspiration to walkers and climbers and those who seek rest and relaxation, it also represents a business interest. The railway which has run up Snowdon since 1896 carries over 140,000 passengers a year. Many passengers plus some of the 200,000 plus walkers a year come for a "view, a brew and a loo" – for Snowdon has a 1930s cafe on its summit, which is infamous for its unsympathetic design. Prince Charles once called it the highest slum in Europe.

The Snowdonia National Park Authority has been exploring the possibility of lottery funding for a new future for the Snowdon Summit. Following consultation the Authority turned away from the original proposal to replace the existing structures with a state of the art visitors' centre on the summit. The input of many different interest groups means that a range of options are now on the table, including minimal development at the summit, with the visitors' centre at the foot of the mountain in Llanberis.

The Snowdon Summit debate involves a classic sustainable development dilemma. The legacy of past generations (building the railway and the cafe in the first place) has compromised the ability of the present generation to enjoy the mountain as it was for many thousands of years and compromises free choice about the mountain's future today.

Bringing thousands of people to a mountain summit, which by its very nature is an inhospitable environment, requires an urban infrastructure to support their supposed needs. These needs have become confused with their expectations – that there will be a cafe and a toilet on top.

The Snowdonia National Park Authority has the opportunity to leave a legacy for future generations that does not compromise what will surely be even more needed in fifty years. Not the need for a brew and a loo (ample facilities already exist at the foot of the mountain), but for the mountain experience. For walkers, this means that if weather conditions are really bad you either do not go or you do not stay long. That would enable better understanding of the mountain ecosystem, and the place of human beings in the natural scheme of things.

The Helvellyn Massif

The Lake District National Park Authority, English Nature and North West Water have joined in a project to find ways of reconciling recreation, conservation and farming management on the Helvellyn Massif. This is one of the most popular areas in the country for walking, with ten car parks providing nearly 600 spaces surrounding it. A thousand people a day make the journey to the summit during the peak Easter and summer periods. Overgrazing had led to ecological damage: an issue for the area's 1993 Environmentally Sensitive Area designation to address.

The project has produced a set of management proposals, on which project partners are consulting. These include better information for visitors about the environmental sensitivity of the area and no new car parks. Proposed research and monitoring includes: the effect of the ESA; hydrology; and the effects of ice climbing.

The emphasis is on protecting the environment and managing visitors and farming use to that end. A land-users forum could be established to discuss the issues.

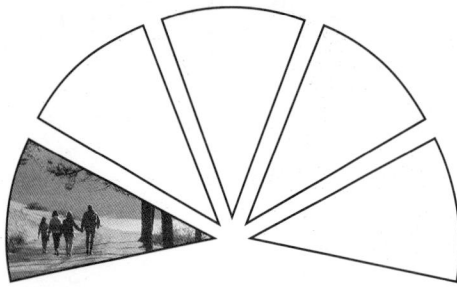

Thousands of tired, nerve shaken people are beginning to find that going to the mountains is going home; that wilderness is a necessity; and that mountain parks and reservations are useful not only as fountains of timber and irrigating rivers, but as fountains of life" (John Muir – Scots born founder of the American environmental movement – 1898, cit. Mountain Agenda-UNCED initiating group 1992). Does Snowdon summit provide the "mountain experience"? Photo: Chris Swan

Section 2: How to measure what we value

"We must find ways of valuing the things that count as well as those that can be counted", Sir Crispin Tickell (chairman of the Government panel on Sustainable Development), to the Friends of the Lake District AGM 1996

Many of the qualities of National Parks do not lend themselves to scientific measurement. They include beauty, tranquillity, remoteness, semi-wilderness and opportunities for quiet enjoyment. The Government's methodology and much of the debate about sustainability has quite understandably tended to focus on what can be counted. For instance, the definition of sustainable development used by the Department of the Environment in its work on environmental indicators implies the measurable: "not only man-made wealth, but also natural wealth, such as clean and adequate water supplies, good arable land, a wealth of wildlife and ample forests" (Department of the Environment 1996b). The culture and purposes of National Parks should have a part to play in enabling the inclusion of other indicators that are not so easily measured, like those mentioned above. National Park values require a different approach that would have many valuable lessons for the whole of the environment.

The history of National Parks brings two traditions together: those who were concerned about the degradation of natural beauty and those who sought quiet enjoyment. The qualities they sought are precisely those that are today missing from the mainstream sustainable development debate.

In the 1920s and 30s environmentalists and those who enjoyed country walking banded together with common concerns about pressures on the countryside. They saw that some of the most beautiful and popular areas were being subjected to "the desecrating hand of modern man" (CPRE 1932). As the Council for the Preservation of Rural England's Sheffield and Peak District Committee observed: "That millions of our people are brought up in surroundings of entire ugliness, is probably the profoundest cause of the spoliation of natural beauty today and the greatest tragedy. For it means that the large part of the population from birth onwards have no standard or knowledge of the beautiful" (op. cit.).

Other concerns were simultaneously being voiced in the Lake District in apocalyptic terms by Rev. H.H. Symonds (1936): "The powers of our mechanism ... the claim of urban needs upon the resources of wild nature and, among the country-born themselves, a higher expectation of the gifts and comfort of science: roads, pylons, motor-coaches, reservoirs: all the harsh, salt, swirling tide of `progress', as it sweeps in a levelling flood across the colour and distinctiveness both of the outer and inner world – these things drive hard against all quietude".

The two notions, of natural beauty and quietude, and the contribution they make to our quality of life, underpin the modern National Parks designation. Those who campaigned for the founding of National Parks sought to preserve those qualities across large areas of the countryside. It is those qualities which National Parks are there to sustain today.

Strategies for Measuring

Measuring the environmental resource of National Parks is a challenge. The National Parks Review Panel supported the value of maps of semi-natural habitat required by Section 3 of the Wildlife and Countryside (Amendment) Act 1985. However, it was concerned that "available environmental data are rarely comprehensive or up-to-date: and that existing National Park plans and Section 3 maps are not drawn widely enough to cover all of the environmental qualities of the Parks". Its key recommendation on this topic was that "National Park Authorities should produce environmental inventories, to be updated and assessed every five years" (Edwards 1991). It said the countryside agencies should prepare guidance on the form and content of such inventories. The Panel said it was vital to monitor trends and identify at an early stage threats to the Parks' integrity and that inventories and research were the main mechanisms for achieving this.

The Monitoring Landscape Change project, involving the countryside agencies and the National Park Authorities, has gone some way to addressing the lack of data. This uses aerial photography to monitor trends like proportions of woodland, moorland, hedgerows etc. Whilst it can monitor general trends, however, it does not involve an evaluation of the quality of the landscape, for instance, the impact of grazing on landscape colour, shape and texture.

The Countryside Commission provided funding for a Sustainability Appraisal of the Plans, Policies and Programmes of the Yorkshire Dales National Park Authority. This concluded that: "the principal task that the Park Authority must now address is the identification of the Park's critical environmental capital and the updating of policies and programmes to secure its long term protection". This would inform the policy objective that: "loss or damage to critical environmental capital is unsustainable and unacceptable" (Baker Associates and Countrywise 1995). This listed the environmental stock to be evaluated and set out a system for surveying and evaluating environmental stock with potentially wide application. **Now is the time for the countryside agencies and the National Park Authorities to address these recommendations on a comprehensive and public basis.**

The countryside agencies have also been involved in a project to set up a monitoring system that would have relevance to all the National Parks. This is being piloted in the North York Moors National Park. This monitoring system is of widespread interest and should involve a wide consultation with National Park communities and voluntary organisations. This could be complemented by the coordinated research programme recommended by the National Parks Review Panel, thus supporting the role of National Parks as test beds for best environmental practice. The Panel stated: "this requires National Park Authorities to understand more clearly how changes of use and management affect the ecological, social and economic systems of the Parks" (Edwards 1991).

An existing vehicle may provide a way of bringing these various ideas and initiatives together and progressing them. The Government's indicators process, involving discussion and consultation, resulted in the publication of a draft set of indicators in 1996. It aims to draw up a set of information on the state of the environment and the factors which impact on it. The Government defines indicators as "quantified information which help to explain how things are changing

over time" (Department of the Environment 1996b).

The Government's methodology involves negative as well as positive indicators – CO_2 emissions as well as environmentally managed land. So in the case of National Parks one would expect to see sites for minerals working alongside dry stone walls, as an indicator of the state of the environment.

The Department of the Environment's indicators report does include the extent of designated areas, including National Parks, as an indicator of sustainable development. But in discussing future indicator development it recognises that this "provides only a partial picture of how well the UK is protecting its important landscapes and habitats". It says: "some measure of the quality and health of these areas is needed to assess whether the situation is getting better or worse" (*op. cit.*).

The Countryside Commission's own Sustainability Appraisal views public consultation as fundamental to this measuring exercise. "The `value' of the countryside depends as much on people's perceptions of what is distinctive and desirable as on technical or scientific knowledge. These value judgements cannot be made without people's involvement and participation" (CAG consultants 1996).

The only designated area for which a "condition-check" is available is the Site of Special Scientific Interest. This can be correlated with National Park boundaries (table 1), although it provides only a very limited picture of the nature of change across a small percentage of the total National Park area, and does not provide an accurate picture of whether change is harmful or not. It is worrying enough that SSSIs in National

Parks are threatened in these ways. **It is evident that before the quality and health of National Parks can be used as an indicator of the environmental health of the nation by the Department of the Environment, some comprehensive groundwork needs to be done.**

The task is to raise National Parks UP the Government's sustainability agenda and integrate them into the national indicators process.

CNP recommends that the countryside agencies, in partnership with the Association of National Park Authorities, work up a comprehensive park-wide set of indicators, a process which would parallel the public consultation being carried out by the Government on this topic. The process should subsequently be fine-tuned to meet each Park's criteria for local distinctiveness.

Once indicators show unsustainable activities and their rate of change, National Park Authorities should set targets (where they have control) to reduce these trends, or encourage others to do so (where they do not have control).

An indicators framework for National Parks must include ways of assessing what is happening to their geomorphology and soil, vegetation and wildlife systems and to their heritage of pre-history and history. In particular:

Natural Beauty

This is undoubtedly the most difficult area and fraught with philosophical as well as practical challenges. However, we can identify the aspects of the natural beauty of an area that people value.

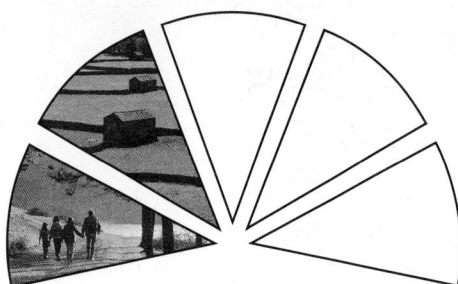

Figure 1   Threatened SSSIs in National Parks

THREAT	BB	B	D	E	LD	N	NYM	P	PC	S	YD
Acid Deposition	4	5	2	5	41	3	8	2		31	6
Overgrazing	1		3		1			1			
Pollution					1						
Development					1			1			
Mineral Extraction	1				1			6		1	2
Agri Drainage								1			
Road Construction	2	1								1	
Rhododendrons										4	
Effluent Pollution		1									
Game Management		1									
Watersports/Boating		1									
Miscellaneous		2		1	2		2	1	4		2
Total Threatened	8	11	5	6	47	3	10	12	4	37	10
Total No. of SSSIs	72	26	41	12	100	32	49	66	65	90	87

Source: Friends of the Earth 1995

Key: BB Brecon Beacons; B Broads; D Dartmoor; E Exmoor; LD Lake District; N Northumberland;
NYM North York Moors; P Peak; PC Pembrokeshire Coast; S Snowdonia; YD Yorkshire Dales

The beauty of the National Parks' landscape is what takes most of us there as visitors and one of the main reasons why National Parks are so highly valued by the nation. The beauty lies both in the broad brush of the land form – its geomorphology – and in the detail of vegetation and features created by humans. From mountains to rolling heather moorland, from mosaics of dry stone walls to wetlands, the Parks embrace many of the landscape features – natural and artificial – that we value in the wilder parts of England and Wales. As the MacEwens (1987) stated, it is "the relative ascendency of the natural world" that characterises much of the National Parks. "We call this characteristic semi-wilderness, and it is from this that the beauty of the Park landscapes is derived". The semi-wild landscapes of National Parks are a precious resource in a country where the majority of the land has been cultivated, drained and fertilised over centuries. The case-studies demonstrate threats to those landscapes and opportunities that exist for enhancement.

Where there are major gaps in landscape types this should be addressed. The family of National Parks should contain a representative gathering of semi-wild landscapes that are both nationally important and locally distinctive. Lowland habitats that offer a sense of the semi-wild over extensive areas should be included in the National Park network for the added protection and opportunities for enhancement the designation provides. The South Downs and New Forest are notable as long recognised candidates.

Case-study 2.1

Lovelier Far

Summary

Within National Parks there is a need to protect the natural beauty from continuing threats and there are also opportunities for enhancement, where past development has left an intrusive legacy.

An old minerals permission

In the Yorkshire Dales National Park, just beside the most scenic part of the Settle to Carlisle Railway in the heart of the popular Three Peaks area, is permission for a quarry to be dug. The two planning permissions that cover the Ribblehead site have existed since the 1950s – just before the Park was designated – and will be in force at the site until 2042, unless the owners, ARC, give them up. The permissions are for 24 hectares of limestone extraction but there has been no significant working at the site for over 20 years. They cover a limestone pavement, designated as a SSSI, and the remains of a Viking settlement. Under the 1995 Environment Act the company would have to produce a set of acceptable conditions before it could start work, but there is nothing in legislation that could take away the permissions without millions being paid in compensation. That is even though such a permission would never be granted today.

A nuclear power station

Permission to build Trawsfynydd Nuclear Power Station in the Snowdonia National Park was given in 1958. The opposition against it at the time called for an alternative site to be found: "in this case the extra cost if any, would be the price for the nation to pay to guard the beauty of the mountains of North Wales" (North Wales Hydro-Electricity Protection Committee leaflet 1958).

Today it no longer produces electricity and the mothballed reactors remain as a legacy of the diminished appetite for nuclear energy. Nuclear Electric, which owns the site, has proposed leaving the eyesore there for 135 years. The company had also identified the option of clearing the site by 2012 with enormous benefits to enhancing the beauty of the area. It has cited economic penalties and technical difficulties amongst the reasons for not supporting the most sustainable – in landscape terms – future for the site. A publicly accountable environmental assessment of options would be an important first step in establishing the most responsible way forward.

The decommissioning of Trawsfynydd nuclear power station provides an opportunity to restore the natural beauty of part of the Snowdonia National Park. Photo: Chris Swan

Section 2

Cultural Heritage

National Parks are cultural landscapes in that the work of humans has helped the natural beauty of the landscape to evolve in the way we value today. The 1995 Environment Act made the conservation and enhancement of cultural heritage specific in the first National Park purpose. Cultural heritage in the National Park context embraces traditional land management practices, the built heritage or uses for local products, many of which derive from sustainable practices.

Cultural heritage can be more broadly defined as "the total experience of a community expressed in a variety of forms – written and collective memory, language, custom, tradition, religion" (Speakman 1992). The conservation of cultural heritage can in many respects equate with the conservation of the environment itself. The Welsh Park Authorities play an important role in encouraging the use of the Welsh language.

One of the key factors that underpins the concept of sustainable development is "intergenerational equity". This means ensuring that future generations have the same resources and the same opportunities for quality of life that we do. Conserving cultural heritage is part of that – it represents the legacy of past generations and helps to answer the question: "what have they left me?"

National Parks, which have been largely safeguarded from obliterative development (although there are threats to the archaeological heritage from farming and forestry practices and military training), have visible evidence of many cultures. The National Parks Review Panel recommended that a comprehensive archaeological database for each National Park

be set up by the various recording agencies. This would provide better information about the environmental stock of the Parks and feed into the indicators process.

The revised first purpose allows National Park Authorities to address the question of cultural heritage in a forward looking way too: "what can we do for future generations?" It allows for enhancement, so that instead of fossilising the culture of the Parks it can evolve in a sustainable way.

Public Understanding and Enjoyment

A 1996 survey by the Countryside Commission found that the overwhelming majority of visitors to National Parks and the New Forest came for the good quality environment to be found there (Countryside Commission 1996a). They enjoyed: scenery and landscape (80%); fresh clean air (68%); peace and quiet (59%).

The Parks provide unparalleled opportunities for the enjoyment of semi-wild and beautiful landscapes: for walking, riding, caving, climbing, cycling, fishing and so on. The purpose of National Parks is to promote opportunities for enjoying the qualities of the Parks: that means enjoyment which depends on the availability of access to those beautiful landscapes. "Within them natural features and processes are dominant and it is still possible to experience the natural world face-to-face with its qualities of wildness and renewal intact" (MacEwens 1987).

The 1995 Environment Act describes the second purpose of National Parks as providing opportunities for understanding and enjoyment of the special qualities of the areas. There is enormous potential for Park Authorities and others who deal with visitors, including voluntary

sector organisations, to drum home a strong environmental message. This would make connections between lifestyles outside the Parks and the degradation of environmental quality in them.

Maintaining public and political support for National Parks is essential as taxpayers' money contributes towards the work of National Park Authorities and environmentally sympathetic farming support. That support has to be constantly revisited and brought to life for every new political generation entering Parliament. So the work of National Park Authorities on public access and interpretation is absolutely vital in maintaining the raison d'etre of National Park designation.

National Park Authorities have many years of experience of plying an environmental message in an enjoyable way – now is the time to redefine and broaden that message for the benefit of National Parks.

Biodiversity

All strategies for Sustainable Development emphasise the need to maintain and enhance biodiversity – the diversity of life on earth. The work of National Park Authorities, with the revised first Park purpose placing a greater emphasis on the conservation and enhancement of wildlife, contributes greatly to the maintenance and enhancement of the nation's stock of biodiversity.

Biodiversity came to public prominence when, in 1992, the UK signed the Convention on Biodiversity at the Earth Summit in Rio. The Government subsequently published the UK Biodiversity Action Plan (UK Government 1994a). From this a Steering Group developed

costed Action Plans and challenged the Government to undertake a comprehensive programme of work (Biodiversity UK Steering Group 1995).

National Park species included in the first set of plans prepared by the Steering Group are identified in Appendix 1. Many actions flow from adoption of the plans. In drawing up the list many National Park Authority ecologists not only identified the species in their areas but also many potential opportunities to re-establish species where they had become rare, isolated or locally extinct. The New Forest and South Downs, candidates for National Park status, contain a significant number of Action Plan habitats and of the species identified in Appendix 1. The need to conserve and enhance their biodiversity harmonises fully with the first purpose of National Parks. **Adding these two areas, which meet the legislative criteria, to the family of National Parks would provide a comprehensive range of habitats, and additional opportunities for enhancement of biodiversity, with great potential for putting the action plans into practice across a wide area.**

The Government gave the Action Plans full support and invited many bodies, including businesses and local government to take up the challenge of putting the plans into practice. National Parks, with their diverse wildlife and many partner organisations, are particularly well placed to take the lead.

The richness of the National Parks in biodiversity is mainly due to their extensive tracts of semi-natural vegetation and associated wealth of species. Habitats range from montane vegetation, peat and fen communities to flower-rich hay meadows. Some areas are

recognised through designation, nationally as SSSIs, or at a European level as Special Protection Areas for birds or candidate Special Areas of Conservation.

Local Biodiversity Action Plans, English Nature's Natural Areas and National Park Management Plans will give a clear focus on options and actions needed for restoring and enhancing the wildlife interest. National Parks farm schemes are one mechanism for fulfilling some of the Action Plans' objectives. Involving more partners – like companies – is the next step and will be decisive in delivering biodiversity.

There is great potential to enhance biodiversity in National Parks:

– by increasing the amount of semi-natural habitat and managing it appropriately eg. management of heather moorland or reedbeds or by withdrawing grazing on moorland and allowing natural succession to take place;

– by cleaning up ecosystems which have become degraded (the Broads Authority's work on phosphate removal is an example);

– by applying pressure to companies or others whose activities affect the biodiversity of National Parks (eg sulphur dioxide emissions from power stations which increase acidification);

– by getting involved in the establishment of a European conservation policy. The Institute for European Environmental Policy has proposed setting up a European ecological network, or "EECoNET", of which National Parks could be a part. This would also be a means to develop international priorities for action in a European context to guide practical conservation measures at a national and local level (Bennett 1991);

– by National Park Authorities taking on a co-ordinating role for the implementation of the biodiversity action plans in the Park. This would mean bringing together other statutory and voluntary bodies, and work on the species and habitats identified as priorities by the UK Steering Group;

– by the new Park Authorities using their powers under the Wildlife and Countryside Act 1981 to prevent damage to species.

Water Resources: Fresh Water

The water bodies of all the National Parks are vital to national environmental sustainability objectives. National Parks represent significant water catchment areas, so water quality and availability are important considerations.

The rivers, lakes and reservoirs of the National Parks are vital sources of supply for urban areas. Much of the water for Manchester and Liverpool is supplied from the Lake District and Peak District. The water is abstracted from lakes and rivers in the Parks and from reservoirs built for the purpose decades ago.

Although there are bore holes near urban areas, water companies often choose the lower cost/higher quality water from National Park sources, without carrying out an assessment of which is the least environmentally damaging source. The subsequent waste of such water through the faltering infrastructure is not consistent with the need to conserve high quality water resources. Increasing demand leads to pressure for abstraction from natural bodies of water, with impacts on their natural beauty and ecology, and possibly in future, to pressure for more reservoirs to be built. In the case of National Parks increased abstraction has

Section 2

implications for recreational use as well.

The water bodies of National Parks are also where a lot of pollutants end up. As elsewhere, there are nitrates from agricultural land and acid rain from power station emissions. Some National Parks are particularly vulnerable to acidification because of the type of soil, so high levels of acid deposition are of particular concern. In some Parks there are also phosphates from sewage treatment works.

Water Resources: Marine

Many National Parks have coastlines and seawater quality is inextricably part of the environmental health of the whole Park. For instance, the coastline off the Snowdonia National Park contains an exceptionally wide variety of ecosystems (Cynefin Environmental Consultants 1996). The Cynefin report commissioned for the National Park Authority found: "the biological richness is due partially to the geographic situation and geological properties of the area, and partly to the relatively low level of environmental pollution".

The Pembrokeshire Coast National Park is also designated as a Heritage Coast, has two coastal National Nature Reserves, a number of coastal SSSIs and, just off the mainland, the Marine Nature Reserve of Skomer. The plethora of designations demonstrates the environmental uniqueness and importance of the area. CNP has long campaigned for a marine extension to the Park with the aim of protecting the whole area as a sustainable ecosystem. The Countryside Council for Wales has called for effective policies for coastal and marine protection to "be applied sufficiently far inland and seawards to allow all resources to be managed" (CCW 1994).

The *Sea Empress* oil tanker disaster in 1996 had a major impact on the ecology and tourism economy of the Pembrokeshire Coast National Park and is discussed more fully in the next section.

Soil

The need to protect and conserve soil resources is gaining increasing prominence, with a chapter devoted to it in the UK Sustainable Development Strategy and a major report by the Royal Commission on Environmental Pollution (RCEP 1996). As agricultural and upland areas, National Parks have a vital role to play as increasing pressures for development fall onto fringe urban areas and agricultural lowland areas. In the light of predictions about global warming, National Parks are likely to become increasingly important as refugia for species under pressure and as areas of food production. Therefore it is vital to protect the soil resources that will assist those changes.

The Royal Commission on Environmental Pollution drew up five principles for policies "to protect soils and ensure the use made of them for all purposes in future is the optimal sustainable use":

– Soils must be conserved as an essential part of life-support systems;

– Soil should be accorded the same priority in environmental protection as air or water;

– An integrated approach to environmental management must include management of land. (That will involve not only giving greater protection to high quality soils and rare ecosystems but recycling previously developed land and severely restricting development on green-field sites);

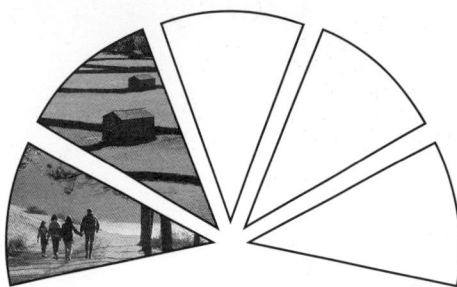

– Contaminated sites should, wherever practicable, be recovered for beneficial use;

– Further contamination of soils from any source should be avoided, whether localised or diffuse.

A fundamental consideration is to minimise further losses of green-field land important for agriculture, conservation and amenity. The proposals for the Otterburn Training Area (case-study 3.7) involve the loss of a substantial area to concrete plus possible increased contamination of soil. The fifth principle on soil contamination should cover land affected by military activity and quarrying. Various road developments proposed for the Parks also involve the loss of green-field sites.

Land in the Lake District between High and Low Newton where a by-pass is to be built. Photo: Chris Swan

Managing rare species and important habitats

Summary

Managing rare species is normally inextricably tied up with the management of the habitat that supports them. National Park Authorities are in a good position to work in partnership with others to manage the ecosystems in which rare species survive and to take a strategic look at the issues that impact upon them. The UK Biodiversity Action Group has prepared action plans for key species which provide a good opportunity for high profile conservation work by the National Park Authorities involved.

Traditional farming practices, like those carried out by Walter Umpleby on his farm in the Yorkshire Dales, help conserve species as well as habitats. The farm has been recently acquired by the National Trust for its nature conservation importance. Photo: Chris Swan

The Broads area supports a number of internationally and nationally important plant species, including the internationally important holly-leaved naiad whose range is spreading thanks to restoration work. The area is also important for otters; the swallowtail butterfly and the bittern. It supports nationally important breeding populations of gadwall and pochard (types of duck) (Holve 1996). All these are targets for management by the Broads Authority and English Nature.

Eggs from the rare fish, the vendace, which is found only in two lakes in the Lake District, are being introduced to lochs in Scotland. This should help secure the long term future of the fish.

The Snowdonia National Park has recently been discovered to be the site of the rare freshwater pearl mussel. Unfortunately it was only after a major population of the mussel had been destroyed accidentally that it was discovered. The Snowdonia National Park Authority has carried out a detailed survey and found only one other site for the mussel. It is now considering reintroducing the mussel to other sites – a long term project that would need many years of monitoring as the mussel lives for up to 60 years. The Park Authority can use its powers under the Wildlife and Countryside Act to prevent further harm to the species.

The lapwing is in decline nationally because of the intensification of agriculture. In the Yorkshire Dales the numbers are falling because of a high density of sheep, supported by Common Agricultural Policy headage payments, increased rolling and harrowing to improve the pasture, a change to rye grass and earlier cutting of grass for silage. All these add up to greater disturbance and a loss of insects that the lapwings eat. The difference is marked: with 20 – 30 birds per square kilometre on Malham Moor and 2 pairs per square kilometre in intensively farmed areas of the Park.

The Yorkshire Dales National Park Authority is encouraging farmers to enter into whole-farm agreements, which aim to plug the gaps left by other environmental schemes, such as the Environmentally Sensitive Area within the Park. The advantage of the whole farm scheme is that it does not encourage the farmer to reduce production in one part of the farm whilst increasing it elsewhere. This allows the lapwing to re-establish itself in areas which have ceased to be suitable for it, as well as surviving on the moorland margins. Although the scheme is limited at present there are hopes that it can be extended widely.

Section 2

Section 3: 2040 vision – unsustainable trends

"Notwithstanding their many achievements, we saw evidence within the Parks of deteriorating environmental quality, permanent damage to the landscape and poor local relationships". National Parks Review Panel (Edwards 1991)

The value of National Parks to strategies for sustainable development is continually under threat from many sources. National economic policies which mitigate against sustainable development (eg the relative costs to the user of private car use and public transport) also impinge on National Parks. Environmentally unsustainable trends may emerge in a piecemeal fashion which are hard to identify until it is too late. They may be major one-off developments that undermine the National Park designation as a whole. They may be specific to National Parks or global trends which have particular impacts on National Parks. They may originate with national or European policies, or relate to the remit of National Park Authorities or simply to the unregulated areas of corporate activity.

This section attempts to identify the most significant, damaging trends.

As any forecaster knows, predicting future outcomes is a high risk activity. For instance, the combined effect may be entirely different from a trend viewed in isolation (eg the mitigating effect of sulphur emissions on global warming) or may have a totally unforeseen effect. This section has simply gathered evidence which today points to trends which need to be addressed now.

Examples of sustainable living which should be promoted and encouraged are identified in the discussion about how to address the issues raised: "A full repairing lease" (Section 5). Any recommendations in this section aim to stop unsustainable practices.

The trends identified below are based on the Countryside Commission's Sustainability Appraisal (CAG consultants 1996) and the Government's seven sins of unsustainability (Secretary of State, John Gummer MP, in a 1993 press statement).

The negative trends that will affect National Parks significantly over the next 50 years are:

- demand for energy;

- intensification and diversification of agriculture;

- increasing demand for aggregates;

- road transport;

- development, including land use changes;

- degradation of water quality;

- demand for water.

The list can be compared with the issues identified 60 years ago by CPRE's Sheffield branch in its report: "The Threat to the Peak" (CPRE 1932):

conifer afforestation; modern buildings; rural advertising; litter; destruction of wildflowers and

bird life; petroleum filling stations; roads; ribbon development; electricity distribution; refuse disposal; industrial development.

That list lacks the global issues that are of such concern today, but many of them are still relevant – we just use different language to describe them. **One thing both lists have in common is the impact they have on the integrity of the Parks. The ex-Director of the American National Park Service, Newton B. Drury recognised this: "If we are going to whittle away at them we should recognise, at the very beginning, that all such whittlings are cumulative and that the end result will be mediocrity. Greatness will be gone".**

Integrity

Sticking drawing pins in the Mona Lisa may only have a localised impact in terms of damage to the painting, but would destroy the integrity of the work of art. All the trends set out in this section attack the integrity of National Parks. Protecting the integrity of the whole area of National Parks should be a priority for the UK Sustainable Development Strategy.

A trend that threatens National Park integrity is the argument by some developers, most notably minerals companies, that trade-offs are possible within National Park boundaries. Applications to extend quarries are "justified" by offers to restore the site with a benefit to the existing National Park environment. Yet future generations may not agree that today's developers and planners were able to enhance important landscapes, like National Parks, by remodelling them to their own tastes and conventions (Mabey 1996). The precautionary principle is a strong component of sustainable development and it should be exercised as much

in relation to land use planning as to pollution control (see case-study 3.1 on trade-offs).

This does not mean that National Parks are "no go" areas for development. That would imply stagnation and fossilisation. The Rural White Paper (DoE/MAFF 1995) promotes a positive approach to development which enhances the character of the countryside, including local distinctiveness: "Wealth creation and environmental quality are increasingly interconnected. In the 21st century environmental quality will offer more economic opportunities than constraints".

Protecting the integrity of National Parks means actively encouraging conservation and enhancement across the whole area. The idea of creating Heritage Areas within National Parks (promoted by the Sandford Committee in 1974) was rejected by the Government, which accepted that the integrity of National Parks was the important factor. The possibility of the conservation and enhancement of natural beauty in Bowness beside Lake Windermere, or in the vicinity of the Hope Valley Cement Works, may seem remote, but it must remain as a policy objective. It is no answer to argue that when interests differ as in the case of the Otterburn Training Area in Northumberland National Park, that area should be removed from the Park. **It is vital to conserve and enhance the whole area that falls inside a National Park boundary, aiming for the highest environmental outcome, even where it does not exist at present (see case-study 3.2).**

Protecting the integrity of National Parks is an important objective in relation to the work being carried out by the Countryside Commission, English Nature and English Heritage on character appraisal.

Section 3

Protecting integrity 1: Landscape trade-offs

Section 3

Summary

Is it possible to decide now on what landscapes and natural environments future generations might need?

In seeking to extend Swinden Quarry in the Yorkshire Dales, the developer, Tilcon, said: "We believe that our plans for the future of Swinden Quarry will make a positive contribution to the unique nature of the Yorkshire Dales National Park ... It will help redress the major shortage of natural wetlands which have been lost over the years through extensive land drainage" (Fit for the Future, Tilcon leaflet).

The successful application by Tilcon was for another 26 years of working at an established quarry in the Dales. This involves the extraction of an extra 37 million tonnes of limestone to below the water table, allowing the hole to be filled with water. Although some of the material is moved by rail, the majority goes by road – 570 heavy lorry movements a day. All but 6% of the material is aggregate – that is crushed rock which could be supplied from other sources.

The application was opposed by many local and national environmental organisations concerned at the lasting and damaging change to a largely unspoilt and typical Dale. "Most of the limestone is being used for road ballast and is rather like using gold to gild the pavements"

(Manchester Area Ramblers, 1995, letter to the Yorkshire Dales National Park Authority). The Secretary of State declined to call in the application, saying it "did not raise issues of more than local importance", even though the mineral did not meet the test of national need with no alternative. The change from typical Dales scenery, the quality of which led to the original National Park designation, to an atypical water-filled crater removes forever the opportunity of future generations enjoying that unique landscape.

The case of Eldon Hill quarry in the Peak District, although a much smaller application, had a similar basis, but a very different outcome. RMC Roadstone, had proposed extending working at the quarry for a further seven years. It placed strong emphasis on the "beneficial landscaping works". It said these would produce "a more open, sympathetic landform" which "would become part of the working rural landscape incorporating new habitats, woodland plantations, and other landscape features representative of its location in the White Peak".

The Peak Park Board rejected the application. It said there was no overriding national need for the mineral and that the proposals "do not represent an overall landscape improvement".

Both the Dales and the Peak Park have landbanks of permitted reserves extending on for several generations. Yet even more permissions are being sought and minerals companies are supporting many applications to extend quarries in National Parks with landscaping arguments. **This compromises the ability of future generations to enjoy the same National Park landscapes as we do – and as hundreds of past generations have done – and locks National Parks into the supply of aggregates for many years ahead.**

Eldon Hill: the company said extending time for working at the quarry would result in it becoming part of the working rural landscape. Photo: Peak Park Board

Protecting integrity 2: it can only get better, or can it?

Summary

Even when areas within National Parks are affected by damaging development or proposals for it, the purposes of designation must prevail. This approach recognises that National Parks are there not just for this, but also for future generations and that the possibility of enhancement must be retained.

Northumberland and the Army

When it became clear that there may be an irreconcilable conflict between Ministry of Defence plans for the Northumberland National Park and its statutory purposes, some members of the House of Lords had an idea: change the National Park boundaries to exclude areas currently used by the Ministry of Defence for military training. This would have the effect of reducing the size of Northumberland by nearly 25%, Dartmoor by 14.5% (right in the centre) and the Pembrokeshire Coast by 4.6% (thus losing the coastal path) as well as lesser proportions of many other Parks.

In moving an amendment to the Environment Bill Lord Annally said: "it makes no sense to re-tie the knot that places the Army's real estate within the jurisdiction of a body which says that its purposes are incompatible with those of military training" (Hansard Vol. 560 No. 34 Col. 1667). The amendment was withdrawn and the importance of the National Park designation to those who own land in them made clear: "If these tracts of land were to be taken out of National Parks the integrity of the whole area would be destroyed so far as management is concerned" (Baroness Nicol, Hansard Vol. 560 No. 34 Col 1672).

Caravans in Pembrokeshire

In 1986 there was an application to turn Meadow House static caravan site in the Pembrokeshire Coast National Park into a site for 163 holiday cottages. The argument in support of the applicant went that, with careful design, the cottages "must improve the present unattractive appearance of the site".

The application was turned down by the National Park Authority which said at the subsequent public inquiry: "it is undeniably the worst possible site on which to start a process of establishing the permanency and acceptability of development, and the conversion to more permanent forms of accommodation and building types". The Countryside Commission supported that view: "whilst the site remains a static caravan site, the possibility remains that at some stage in the future it will be cleared and will return to the state ... it should have been left in. Once buildings are put upon it to the extent that is contemplated, the possibility is gone forever". The Inspector and the Secretary of State agreed.

Both of these examples clarify the persisting nature of the designation and its purposes over the whole of the Park area, compared with the transience of manifold land uses within the Park boundary.

Military training in Northumberland National Park

Section 3

Unsustainable trend 1: demand for energy

Climate Change

Predictions on climate change are fraught with uncertainty. The latest report of the UK Climate Change Impacts Review Group (UKCCIRG 1996) predicted that climate change over the next 30 years will push climate zones northwards by 120 miles. Its predictions include temperatures rising by about 0.2°C each decade, more frequent warm seasons and years, a 10% increase in rainfall by the 2050s, higher wind speeds and sea level rising at the rate of about 5cm per decade.

Global warming is caused or enhanced by a build up of greenhouse gases. The UK has a target to reduce emissions of such gases by 5-10 per cent of 1990 levels by 2010. Environmental organisations are pressing for a reduction of CO_2 by at least 20% of 1990 levels by 2005 in order to address the problem meaningfully (letter by Climate Action Network to the Independent, 5th July 1996).

The Countryside Commission examined the question in its 1995 report, Climate Change, Acidification and Ozone (Countryside Commission 1995). The Commission makes the point that place-specific projections are impossible at this stage. Based on the Commission's work and the latest Government findings (UKCCIRG 1996) the following predicted trends would impact on National Parks:

– soil loss – significantly for National Parks, wetlands and peat soils are at particular risk from drying and wind erosion

– migration of agriculture to higher altitudes – this could put pressure on upland areas for more intensive forms of agriculture, including cereal production, with a loss of semi-natural vegetation and access opportunities

– vegetation change – significantly for National Parks "some wet, montane and coastal communities will be lost" (DoE 1996). Likely to result in significant loss of biodiversity: many currently endangered species are threatened

– increased fire risk which could reduce access opportunities at danger times

– a rise in sea level which will lead to more coastal erosion, (already a problem for the North York Moors National Park), the loss of some lowland habitats, like parts of the Broads (a 19cm increase is predicted by 2020 and 37cm by 2050) and exacerbation of coastal squeeze

– more demand for water, especially for irrigation, and changing water gathering patterns may mean pressure for more reservoirs and abstraction in National Parks

– reduced water quality, eg an increased incidence of toxic algal blooms associated with warmer weather

– more holidays likely to be taken in the UK with resulting increased visitor pressure on National Parks, particularly on coastlines, lakes and rivers

– as climate change comes about it is likely that pressure for increased renewable energy generation and energy conservation may lead to more landscape impacts (eg from large wind power stations) or affect local design traditions (eg where energy conservation features are visible on buildings)

If demand for energy continues to rise there may be increasing pressure for cheaper and more polluting fuels, like orimulsion or Pett coke. These are both overseas imports which, it has already been proposed, will be burnt in English and Welsh power stations.

Although the problems of energy demand may seem too enormous to tackle except at Government level, National Parks do have a role to play. This is discussed in detail in the agenda on energy.

Section 3

Case-study 3.3

Waving or drowning?

Summary

Because of the potentially significant impacts on National Parks of climate change, it has been suggested that contingency planning should begin now. The Broads Authority has already started planning to manage the predicted changes, including a rise in sea level.

Forecast rises in sea level are attributed to global warming and the tilting of the British Isles, downwards towards the south (UKCCIRG 1996). Over the next 50 years Government scientists predict a 20 – 30 cm increase in sea level because of climate change. The Broads area, which lies at sea level in East Anglia, is recognised as a wetland of international importance for nature conservation. It has 27 Sites of Special Scientific Interest, making up 20% of the Broads. These areas are also designated as Ramsar sites (internationally important wetlands) and Special Protection Areas (designated under the EC Birds Directive) and are candidates for the new European Special Area of Conservation (SAC), designation.

Before the 13th century the area was a "fully functioning wetland, with the whole of the floodplain acting as a single unit and demonstrating an unfettered transition from sea to freshwater" (Holve H. 1996). Extensive peat extraction in the middle ages, fen harvest and grazing helped to shape today's mixed habitat. It has been subject to changes in relative sea level and saltwater intrusion in the past but these changes have occurred over long timescales. Climate change is likely to mean dramatic short term changes with low rivers in summer and wetlands competing with agriculture and public supply for water, plus the increased risk of flooding for drained marshland and properties in the floodplain.

The Broads Authority can pursue one of two courses of action: to try to preserve the Broads as they are by increasingly intensive water management and building tidal defences or by managing the change over time. The latter approach is favoured by the Broads Authority and English Nature in their advisory document on nature conservation and would mean allowing "as much time as possible for valued freshwater systems to adjust to a new equilibrium and for the creation of alternative habitats elsewhere" (op. cit). Its flood defence programme aims to accommodate the changes ahead, keeping a transition of a salt to freshwater ecosystem.

Either way it is clear that the options are expensive and risky and that there will be significant losses of the existing habitat from saltwater incursion.

Carr woodland in the Broads would be threatened by intrusion of saltwater

Section 3

Unsustainable trend 2:
acidification

Unsustainable trend 2: acidification

Acid deposition from burning fossil fuels, mainly in power stations but also from road transport, affects the quality of air, soils and water. It reduces biodiversity and increases soil erosion although its full effects are not known and are the subject of much research. There is concern about the effect of acid pollution on semi-natural vegetation, like moorland, because it is known that blanket bogs have been damaged by deposition of sulphur and nitrogen. The health of forests has also been studied in relation to acid deposition and there is evidence of increased acidification of some soils, resulting in changes in soil biology. The changes are likely to alter plant nutrition and to change the chemistry and biology of freshwaters (INDITE 1994). Increased acidification may also exacerbate the problems associated with overgrazing (see next section).

Some National Parks are particularly vulnerable because their fragile upland soils are much less able to withstand the acidification as well as receiving high levels of acid deposition. Some soils, eg the podzols of north west Wales, have already become saturated with sulphate and further deposition of sulphate leads to increases in acidity and aluminium concentrations in drainage waters (op. cit.). "Coniferous forests, thin soils on rocks with little bases (mainly lime) and lake and river waters with a low pH are at great risk" (Countryside Commission 1995).

Whilst emissions of sulphur dioxide (SO_2) are falling (DOE 1996) and new targets have recently been agreed, emissions of oxides of nitrogen (NO_x) have not been falling as quickly, mainly because of the increase in road transport (see figure 2). However the Government predicts a fall in NO_x emissions because of increased use of diesel cars, increased road fuel duty and the introduction of catalytic converters.

Changes in fuel burnt in power stations may affect these trends. A proposal to burn the high-sulphur fuel orimulsion at Pembroke Power Station would increase SO_2 emissions from the station by 62% and NO_x by over 500% compared with 1996 (not at full load) emission levels, even after flue-gas desulphurisation. This could have far reaching effects.

Research for the Joint Nature Conservation Committee (JNCC 1996) found that power station location was an important factor in determining the impact of its emissions on SSSIs.

This means that even relatively small acid emissions from some power stations can have a large impact, simply because of where they are in relation to sensitive areas.

Section 3

Figure 2 Acid emissions

Source: Environment Statistics No. 18: 1996 (HMSO)

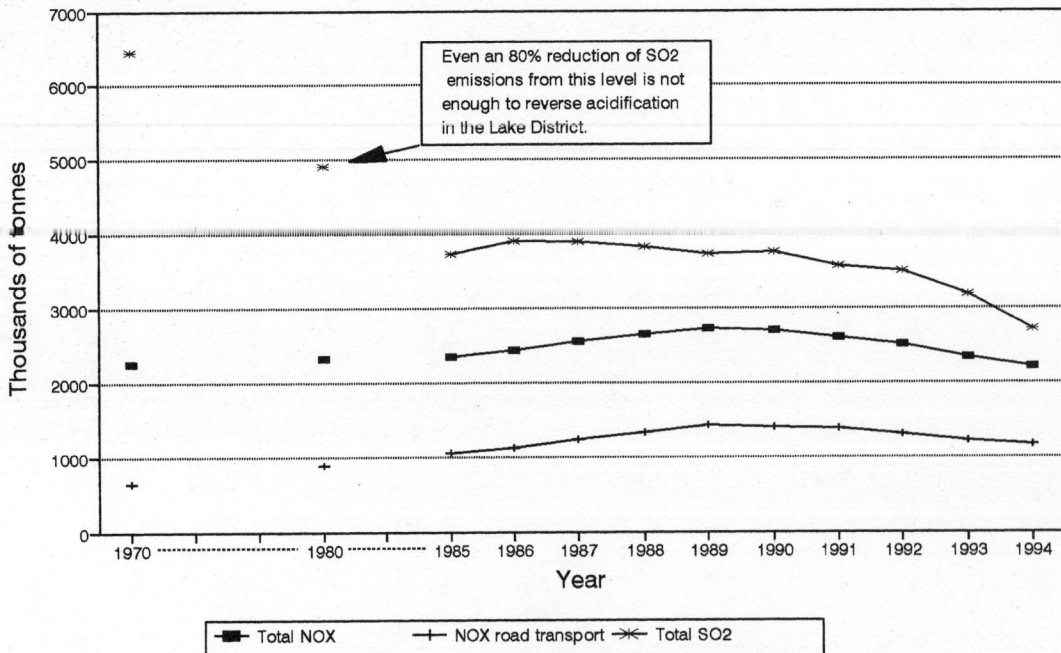

Even an 80% reduction of SO2 emissions from this level is not enough to reverse acidification in the Lake District.

Thousands of tonnes

Year

Total NOX   NOX road transport   Total SO2

Case-study 3.4

Acid terns and lichens in the Lake District

Summary

Some of the most serious trends affecting National Parks originate outside the Parks and outside the normal spheres of influence of the Park Authorities. Major reductions in sulphur and nitrogen emissions are needed before acidification in sensitive areas of the Lake District can be reversed.

The Lake District is one of the National Parks most vulnerable to acidification (because of the nature of the soil) and where acid deposition is high (high rainfall brought on air flows from industrial areas).

A study of freshwater tarns near Wastwater in the Lake District was carried out by the Institute of Freshwater Ecology. It looked at sediment samples, going back 1,000 years. Evidence of pollution from industrial sources was found starting in the nineteenth century. More rapid acidification and a build up of heavy metals have been going on since the 1950s "correlated with the steep increases in atmospheric pollution" (Haworth and Lishman 1991).

The work has been taken forward by a study modelling what might happen in the tarns in future (Whitehead *et al.* unpublished 1996). The study includes the effect new sulphur reduction protocols adopted by the UK might have on reversing the effects of past pollution (see footnote). It found that "even an 80% sulphate reduction will be insufficient to achieve long term sustained reversibility of acidification in sensitive catchments such as Scoat Tarn." This is because of the increases in nitrate emissions from vehicles. Lower reductions would mean the tarns taking even longer to recover.

The effect of acid deposition is not limited to the freshwater environment. Another indicator in the Lake District is the internationally important lichen communities found in National Trust woodlands in Borrowdale. The genus *Lobaria*, which is a group of especially large and distinctive lichens, is particularly sensitive to acidification. Studies have shown a long-term decline in the vigour of these lichen communities, with acid deposition the most likely cause (Farmer *et al.* 1991). Certain species have already disappeared from Borrowdale. A paper (1992) to the Lake District National Park Board states: "Borrowdale highlights the need for controls over emissions to be realised if the lichen communities and other damaged habitats are to be given a chance to recover".

The Lake District National Park Authority does support research on acidification but has expressed concern that its influence on controlling emissions is limited. The role of National Park Authorities in this wider arena is discussed in the agenda on energy.

Borrowdale Woods: The Lungwort lichen (Lobaria pulmonaria) threatened by acid deposition in the Lake District. Photo: Chris Swan

Footnote: Under the terms of the second UNECE Sulphur Protocol, the UK is committed to reducing national emissions of sulphur dioxide by 80% by 2010 compared with 1980 levels.

Section 3

Unsustainable trend 3: intensive agriculture and forestry

Intensive use of the land for agricultural production started just before the Second World War and can be seen today in the cereal monocultures of east Anglia and the heavily grazed hills in some National Parks. Agricultural support, until recently geared up to supporting ever increasing production, is often directly at odds with sustainable land management which has been practised over thousands of years. Although a very large percentage of National Park land is now in some kind of agri-environment scheme, farmers in upland areas on marginal lands still often rely on payments based on the number of livestock they have. The move from subsidy-led farming support to incentives for environmentally friendly farming would need to be expanded and developed to encourage many farmers to manage their holdings differently.

The Government has introduced some so-called agri-environment schemes, although the ability of these to offset the environmental degradation caused by the production-driven Common Agricultural Policy (CAP) is small (spending on them equates with 4% of total spending on the CAP). These incentive-led schemes include: the Environmentally Sensitive Areas scheme; Countryside Stewardship in England; Tir Cymen in Wales; National Park Farm Schemes and the Wildlife Enhancement Scheme. These forms of support have allowed major environmental gains in some places. It is significant, however, that large areas of some National Parks are not designated as Environmentally Sensitive Areas and do not fall into the Countryside Stewardship, Tir Cymen or other schemes.

Loss of semi-natural habitat can be traced in National Parks since they were designated. In 1954 heather moorland covered about a third of the Exmoor National Park area – in 1987 it covered a fragmented quarter (A. and M. MacEwen 1987). A monitoring project on landscape change in National Parks in the 1970s – 1980s (Countryside Commission 1991) found an increase in the total area of cultivated land, improved pasture and coniferous forest and in the length of fences. There was a decrease in semi-natural areas, such as moor and heath, in rough pasture and in traditional features of the landscape, such as hedgerows and walls (see figure 3: source Countryside Commission 1991). A Government survey from 1990 showed, between 1984 and 1990, a decrease in managed hedgerow of 23% and, between 1978 and 1990, significant losses of wild flower rich grassland (cit. MAFF 1995). Any further losses of these already depleted natural resources to agricultural use or other development are critical indeed.

The Government survey found a 3% increase in broadleaved woodland between 1984 and 1990. However, this should be set against losses of ancient woodland to agriculture – Dartmoor has lost 77 hectares this century.

The Royal Commission on Environmental Pollution (1996) identified soil erosion related to sheep grazing as a particularly serious problem. It found that since the 1940s the number of sheep in the Peak District and Wales had increased threefold. Research by the National Rivers Authority (reported in the Geographical Magazine June 1996) found that a 40% increase in sheep numbers in the Yorkshire Dales was linked to recent flooding. The 1995 flood was the highest since records began in 1862. The overgrazing leads to loss of vegetation, more trampling and reduced water infiltration. Rain then runs off, rather than soaking into the soil. The overgrazing was also found to lead to riverbank erosion and water pollution.

Overall, the evidence from around the Parks is of:

– selective stewardship – so that some areas or features within the holding are conserved whilst more intensive production takes place elsewhere

– more intensive farmers/owners outbidding less intensive farmers for vacant land, leading to agricultural intensification of what may have been land of conservation value

– reduction in the practice of shepherding which normally manages grazing levels

– greater frequency of all-year round grazing, by using supplementary feed

– increased pollution of water courses (see below) in run off from heavily stocked areas and from dairying in upland areas

– increased flooding risk due to overgrazing

– intensively farmed soil becoming more susceptible to erosion (eg from walkers)

– loss of heather, whortleberries and other typical heather moorland species and an increase in other species (eg bent/fescue grasses)

– loss of upland heather moorland is related to a decrease in the diversity of bird species

– the replacement of semi-natural habitats with farmland in intensive production which represents a significant loss to National Parks and to their visitors

– clear felling and replacement of conifer plantations as they reach the end of their rotations (see the

Section 3

case-study on forestry futures)

Action to address most of these problems is being taken across the Parks and the results can be speedy and gratifying. These initiatives are discussed in the land management agenda, which looks at opportunities for positive action. "Preventing further losses of heather moorland and encouraging regeneration of dwarf shrubs in areas of degraded moorland is not difficult. Around 80% of the heather moorland lost or damaged in England and Wales since 1947 has some potential for recovery with improved management" (Countryside Council for Wales 1995). The Royal Commission on Environmental Pollution was also heartened by the speed of recovery. On National Trust land in the Peak District where sheep stocking levels had been reduced in 1983 it found that "the proportion of bare ground has declined dramatically and heather and bilberry are once again becoming dominant on previously badly eroded areas" (RCEP 1996). However some elements of the habitat may take much longer to re-establish.

CNP supports the RCEP recommendation that the agriculture departments put research in hand to explore how far erosion of upland peat could be halted or reversed by changes in land use practices and suggests that National Parks, as testbeds for sustainable practices, would be a good place to start.

National Park Authorities should also be given a "last stop" power, where a Conservation Order could be made to stop damage to features of high conservation value and/or recreational importance.

National Park Authorities could also consider a rolling programme of acquiring land of high conservation value, with a view to resale, with a covenant in place that requires environmentally sensitive management (the Peak Park Board has done this for small woodlands).

Case-study 3.5

Forestry futures

Summary

The National Parks Review Panel (Edwards 1991) recommended that full advantage should be taken of "opportunities, provided by the second rotation, to improve the environmental qualities of forested areas in the National Parks". The future of Alport Dale in the Peak National Park raises a number of relevant issues.

The original set of proposals by Forest Enterprise to clear fell and replant its plantations at Alport Dale were so controversial that they have become the focus of a "Hands Off Alport Dale" campaign. No planning permission is required but Forest Enterprise has consulted the National Park Authority. Most of Alport Dale is a SSSI and lies in a Special Protection Area for Birds.

Just over 100 hectares of woodland have been established at Alport Dale since 1930 and the plan was to

harvest and replant the mature plantations. The first set of plans, which included upgrading unmade roads and building a stretch of new road, were the focus of bitter opposition. There were concerns about the impacts on landscape character, ecology, archaeological interest and on recreational enjoyment. 3,000 tons of timber would have been removed by heavy lorries every five years.

A sustainable future for Alport Dale could now emerge as a result of concerns about the original set of proposals. The environmental assessment process allows for all options to be considered. It would include an assessment of the impacts of options on water quality, landscape, soil and so on as well as timber production. It would allow a vision of the future plantation to be established, which would enhance the National Park and its environment in an enduring way.

Figure 3 Landscape change in National Parks
(Between 1970s and 1980s)

Change	B	BB	D	E	LD	N	NYM	P	PC	S	YD
Cultivated land km2	+36	+7	+8	+1	+33	+4	+8	+3	+4	-	0
Broad leaf woodland km2	+4	-2	-	0	0	0	+3	+1	+1	+2	0
Coniferous woodland km2	-	+2	0	+6	+11	+30	+3	+5	-	+43	+6
Hedgerow length km	-11	-150	-119	-343	-186	0	-198	-42	-58	-95	-10
Upland heath km2	-	-7	-1	-5	+2	-16	+3	-3	-3	-16	+3
Improved pasture km2	-18	*a	-5	*a	*a	*a	-1	*a	*a	+27	+24
Rough pasture km2	-18	-10	-3	-5	-32	-3	-2	-2	-3	-26	-29
Fencing km	+10	+3	+32	+64	+49	+14	+91	+14	+9	+41	-20
Walls length km	-	0	-3	+2	-11	-16	-80	-230	-	-54	-20
Grass moor km2	-	-6	+2	*b	-	-15	0	-2	*b	-26	-4
Coastal heath km2	-	-	-	-	+11	-	+1	-	-1	+4	-
Blanket peat moor km2	-	-	-	-	-	-	-	-2	-	-	-
Bracken km2	-	+7	-2	-5	-13	-1	-3	0	-1	-3	0
Freshwater marshes km2	-2	-	-	-	+1	-	-	-	-	-	-
Developed Land km2	+1	0	+2	0	+2	0	+1	0	0	+3	+2
Ditches km	+138	-	-	-	-	-	-	-	-	-	-
Open Water km2	+1	-	-	+2	-	0	-	0	-1	+2	+1
Banks km	-	-	-	+110	-	-	-	-	-67	-	-

Notes to figure 3: a = included with cultivated land figure, b = included with rough pasture figure

Key: B Broads; BB Brecon Beacons; D Dartmoor; E Exmoor; LD Lake District; N Northumberland; NYM North York Moors

P Peak; PC Pembrokeshire Coast; S Snowdonia; YD Yorkshire Dales

Section 3

Case-study 3.6

Grazing on common land

Overgrazing is a real problem on the upland areas of many of the Parks, particularly on common land where there may be many users. Overgrazing leads to loss of heather and its associated species, with grasses and possibly bracken replacing the heather, and increased risk of soil erosion. On common land neither the owner of the soil nor the commoners have the individual right to manage the land. Under existing law individual commoners cannot be prevented from exercising full grazing rights. Only if all the commoners agree can numbers of livestock be controlled or other land management improvements be introduced.

This is a major issue in those National Parks where there is a large proportion of common land (figure 4). For instance Armboth Fell in the Lake District is covered by an Environmentally Sensitive Area (ESA) designation with the main purpose of reducing the number of sheep on the fells. But it is common land, owned by the National Trust, where no general agreement has been reached about numbers. Fencing has been put up to encourage heather regeneration, in lieu of management by farmers, but this is itself a serious issue in an open moorland area.

One alternative to fencing on open areas and common land is the reintroduction of shepherding (perhaps using agri-environment money to employ people on the hills again).

In the Dartmoor National Park heather has disappeared comparatively recently on some areas of common land at Ugborough and Gidleigh. The agriculture departments are attempting to address this trend by withholding livestock payments where the vegetation cannot support the number of stock without deterioration. It is as yet too early to assess the effectiveness of this rule but it removes the subsidy incentive which has led to overstocking. The 1985 Dartmoor Commons Act tried to establish a management agreement for the Dartmoor commons as well as giving walkers and riders the right to walk and ride on all the Dartmoor commons.

The Royal Commission on Environmental Pollution's report on soil recommends "that the Government expedite changes in the law applying to common land". It supports the proposal that where 75% of commoners who exercise their rights are in favour, schemes can be agreed.

The Council for National Parks supports the recommendations of the Common Land Forum (Countryside Commission 1986). At the time of its publication the Countryside Commission stated: "the future of common land law passes to the Government". This opportunity to agree a sustainable future for common land has still not been taken ten years on.

Recommendations:

introduce national legislation on common land to include measures to improve the management of commons (especially to enable the use of model management schemes on common land in National Parks).

The Common Land Forum described the purpose of any such management scheme to be:

"to continue the exercise of commoners and owners rights in or over the common; to maintain the common and to promote proper standards of livestock husbandry thereon; and to promote the conservation and enhancement of the natural beauty of the common and access to it by persons for the purpose of quiet enjoyment" (Countryside Commission 1986).

The Forum recommended that management associations should be formed for each common and model schemes be drawn up for grazing and amenity commons. After five years allowed for drawing up the schemes all commons would be open to public access on foot for quiet enjoyment. A key role for National Park staff is to work with common land associations (where they exist) to implement the management agreements (the Brecon Beacons National Park Authority's Meithrin Mynydd project addresses this issue).

In the absence of legislation it would be helpful to target existing measures to improve the management of grazing (eg under ESAs/Tir Cymen) on common land.

The National Park Authorities should continue to press the government to implement the Common Land Forum proposals, including those relating to public right of access, and should do their utmost to assist the Department of the Environment in preparing its best practice guide for the management of common land.

Figure 4 Percentage of common land in National Parks

National Park	% Common land
Broads	Virtually nil
Brecon Beacons	35%
Dartmoor	39%
Exmoor	7%
Lake District	27%
Northumberland	Virtually nil
North York Moors	55%
Peak	Small, in isolated areas
Pembrokeshire Coast	6%
Snowdonia	Just over 10%
Yorkshire Dales	29%

Source: Council for National Parks survey 1996

Section 3

Unsustainable trend 4: Increasing demand for aggregates

National Parks supply many kinds of minerals – but the vast majority are crushed to produce aggregates (for a variety of construction uses). This is a use for which there are many alternative, lower grade sources. Planning tests mean that there should be a very strong presumption against mineral development in National Parks. Minerals Planning Policy Guidance Note 6 (for aggregates' provision) states that such development "should not take place in these areas" ... "save in exceptional circumstances". Criteria for assessment include two key questions: whether there is a national need for the development and whether there are alternatives (including meeting the need in another way). Despite this, the original ten National Parks, which cover 9 per cent of the land area of England and Wales, produce at least as high a proportion of our construction aggregates as anywhere else.

The reasons for this go back decades as many of the current permissions pre-date the designation of the Parks. Restructuring and consolidation by minerals companies in the 1990s has tended to concentrate production onto the big, established quarries, many of which are in the Parks.

Today, if any National Park quarry is nearing the end of its life, the operator seeks an extension in return for landscaping the site afterwards. Although it is true that it would be unlikely for any major new quarry to be given permission in a National Park today, the impact from extensions to existing quarries – both to the landscape and from the day to day quarrying operation – is no less. It is a hard fact that it is easier to get permission for a bigger quarry in a National Park than on a green field site anywhere else, regardless of the environmental value of the green field site or the scope for restoration.

This adds up to:

– a level of supply of aggregates that is becoming increasingly hard to sustain in landscape terms

– a trend of extending existing mineral workings in National Parks, where the shape of the landscape in the future is being largely dictated by minerals companies rather than the planning system

There are two strategies for addressing this:

– managing demand for minerals

– environmentally-led land provision for aggregates working

The revised Minerals Planning Guidance Note 6 for England (Department of the Environment 1994) addressed both these points. It said the need for roads, buildings and so on should be met "in ways which demand less use of aggregates". It said remaining demand should be met by a shift away from traditional, land-won sources of aggregates. But the new emphasis placed on marine dredged sand and gravel and superquarries has its own environmental problems. In the case of National Parks, the Pembrokeshire Coast supplies marine sand and gravel and Tunstead is a superquarry straddling the boundary of the Peak Park. In the absence of management of the demand for aggregates and with a system led by the "predict and provide" approach of the Regional Aggregates Working Parties it is not enough simply to shift the burden.

The Government is committed to substituting the supply of primary aggregates with recycled and waste aggregates, where possible. The full scope for this substitution, including its relation to individual planning decisions, has yet to be determined. Yet National Parks are locked into supplying primary aggregates for generations – in the Brecon Beacons and Pembrokeshire Coast, reserves of all rocks would last 35 years (Green Balance 1993). These Parks have 24 million tonnes of permitted rock reserves waiting to be worked in dormant quarries. There is enormous slack in the system with so many permissions already given. This is a fact that should be exploited to advantage by minerals companies, minerals consumers, Government policy and National Park Authorities when planning ahead for further or extended mineral working.

Figure 5 shows the extent of mineral working in National Parks.

The Peak Park Board attempted to address the whole question of future supply of minerals when drawing up its last Structure Plan (see case-study 3.6).

Section 3

Croes-y-Ddwy-Afon slate quarry in a Site of Special Scientific Interest near Ffestiniog in the Snowdonia National Park: landscaping bonds would help guarantee restoration. This quarry, owned by the Crown Estate, has lain derelict since the company which had the permission went out of business. Photo: Chris Swan

Unsustainable trend 4:
Increasing demand for
aggregates

Case-study 3.7

Aggregates: Making a stand

The Peak National Park accounts for 38% of all mineral activity in National Parks by area and by number of sites. It is the country's principal supplier of the vein mineral fluorspar and supplied well over 8.6 million tonnes of aggregates in 1990 for use in construction and industrial applications. This compared with 3.9 million tonnes in 1981. At the rate of sale in 1989, the permitted reserves of limestone in the Peak District would last for 47 years and sandstone for 112 years. Quarries within the Park produce about 26% of the total aggregates extraction in the East Midlands region.

In 1994 the Peak National Park Authority revised its Structure Plan and did not include provision for a minerals land bank. This is a stock of permitted minerals reserves for a particular area over a defined period. At that time the requirement was for a land bank for crushed rock to be maintained at 10 years. The Park Authority argued that: "National Parks are not the same as counties and districts elsewhere. There is a statutory duty under the National Parks Act to conserve and enhance their natural beauty... In any case a `landbank' is already provided for by existing planning permissions

– many dating back to the 1950s or even earlier. There is no need for further provision, while allowing for additional quarrying would certainly result in serious damage to the environment" (Cllr Martin Doughty, Peak Park chairman in a press release 3 December 1993).

The Department of the Environment insisted that a landbank should be provided for. It said the Board should have regard to the need to maintain a landbank "in considering proposals for mineral extraction".

The Peak Park Authority was quite right to take this principled position. Making the supply of minerals from National Parks truly determined by exceptional need would require removing National Parks from the landbank system. This would help break the historical pattern of supply from National Parks and allow planning for minerals supply in the future to be led by the minerals planning authorities, rather than demand determined elsewhere.

Figure 5 Mineral working in National Parks

Park	Area covered by mineral permissions (ha)	Number of surface minerals workings		Estimated proportion of aggregates (%)
		Active	Dormant	
BB	364	6	15	>90%
B	76	2	0	100%
D	64	5	8	90%
E	0	0	0	n/a
LD	172	17	3	Not known
N	53	4	1	99%
NYM	74	4	3	98%
P	1,498	57	13	Not known
PC	62	7	1	100%
S	53	3	5	>95%
YD	1,692	11	6	97.8%

Source: CNP 1996 survey

Key: BB Brecon Beacons; B Broads; D Dartmoor; E Exmoor; LD Lake District; N Northumberland

NYM North York Moors; P Peak; PC Pembrokeshire Coast; S Snowdonia; YD Yorkshire Dales

In 1992 research for the Countryside Commission predicted a fourfold increase in traffic on rural roads by 2025 (Countryside Commission 1992). Figure 6 shows recent growth in road traffic, starting from the recession in the early 1980s and the Government's forecast of a 142% increase on present figures by 2025. National Parks already carry a heavy burden of rural traffic. Not only do residents, like many other rural dwellers, lack access to public transport, but many visitors arrive by car. This not only causes localised traffic jams and parking problems – in towns and villages or at popular sites – but increases pressure for car users to be catered for. There is also a problem with through traffic in some Parks. For instance, the Peak District carries several main trans-Pennine routes and the A470 south to north Wales route passes through the Brecon Beacons and the Snowdonia National Parks. The minerals extraction industry also brings hundreds of heavy lorry movements to the Parks.

These factors mean pressure for:

– dualling and straightening of roads, making them more urban in character and allowing faster traffic;

– by-passes across the countryside;

– more car parks in towns and villages, near popular attractions and in the countryside;

– more urban-style street furniture (signs, lighting, road markings etc).

Traffic management schemes, discussed in more detail in Section 5, are now being drawn up in many National Parks.

It is not just the traffic in National Parks that has an effect – there are other pressures to do with road transport which may originate far away.

Demand for minerals

Road building, upgrading and resurfacing all use minerals – many from National Parks. 24% of all primary aggregates go for roads (Ecotec research cit. Department of the Environment 1994). National Parks not only supply general aggregates but also high quality materials for road surfaces. There is a direct link between the road building programme and the rate and scale at which minerals in National Parks are worked.

Atmospheric Pollution

Traffic emissions not only contribute to global warming, described above, but also give rise to other pollutants (NO_x and volatile organic compounds), which, combined with sunlight, produce low level ozone. Although much of this pollution originates in urban areas, rural and particularly upland areas are badly affected by it. The map on the next page (figure 7) clearly shows high levels of ozone affecting the two Parks in the south west, the three Parks in Wales, the Peak Park, the Yorkshire Dales and the North York Moors.

The effects of low level ozone include reduced visibility (blue haze or smog) and eye irritation: "coupled with the associated reduction in visibility, it will certainly lead to less enjoyment of the uplands on affected days and may even lead to a reduction in high altitude walking on the hottest days of summer" (Countryside Commission 1995).

Section 3

Figure 6 Road traffic growth

Source: Transport statistics Great Britain 1995 (HMSO)

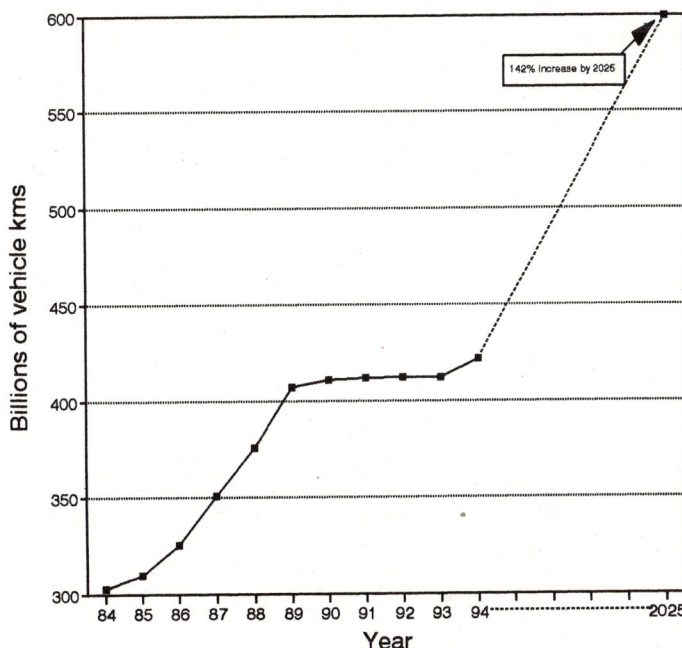

142% increase by 2025

Billions of vehicle kms

Year

Figure 7 Ozone map

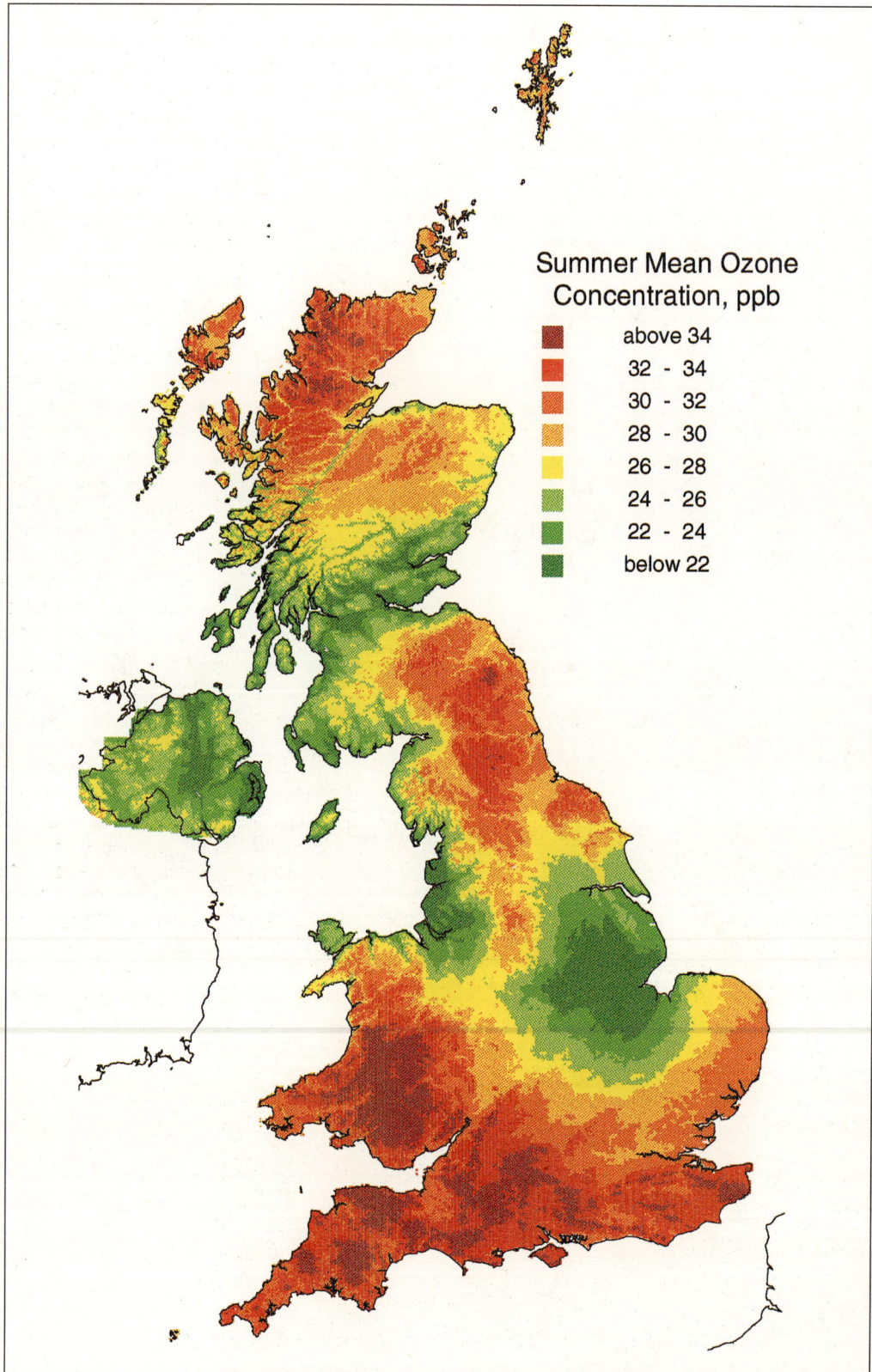

Summer Mean Ozone Concentration, ppb

- above 34
- 32 - 34
- 30 - 32
- 28 - 30
- 26 - 28
- 24 - 26
- 22 - 24
- below 22

source: DoE, Third Report of the United Kingdom Photochemical Oxidants Review Group, 1993.

Section 3

Unsustainable trend 6: development

National Parks are, perhaps surprisingly, under greater pressure than many other rural areas and some urban areas for development. National Park Authorities act as the development control authority for all proposals, including county matters like waste and minerals development. The total number of decisions made by English National Parks in 1995 is shown in figure 8. The number has been compared with a neighbouring rural area and a nearby urban area and presented as numbers of planning applications per 1,000 people. In nearly all cases National Parks received far more planning applications than neighbouring local authorities.

The demand for development, in particular housing, is predicted to rise dramatically over the next 30 years. The Government's projections suggest 4.4 million extra households in England with most of the demand being met on greenfield sites (Department of the Environment/MAFF 1995). The projections indicate that an area of rural England larger than Greater London will disappear.

There are also pressures from infrastructure developments like roads (discussed above), energy and telecommunications transmission lines and masts and renewable energy technologies. Many problems associated with these are associated with an absence of control under the planning system (eg carriageway signing). There is also the lack of a framework to discuss or challenge need (eg full coverage by mobile phone along A-class roads in the Parks) before individual applications are put forward.

Whilst there may be significant benefits for certain sustainability objectives from renewable energy (eg reduced reliance on fossil fuels), the technologies involved can conflict with National Park purposes. The impact of a large scale wind power station on an open upland area means fundamental change to the landscape with the potential for long-lasting degradation in landscape quality. Some hydro electric schemes can also permanently degrade the ecology and landscape of National Parks. In National Park terms developments on such a scale must be considered unsustainable as must the cumulative impact of many smaller schemes in some locations.

Changes in the use of National Parks – for instance by the kind or intensity of military activity or by changes in the nature of recreational pursuits (eg dependence on motorised vehicles for off-road activities) – also have effects. These may not require planning permission but can involve lasting impacts to National Park qualities.

The Cwm Dyli water pipeline in Snowdonia for hydro-electric power intrudes onto the natural beauty of the mountain massif. Photo: Chris Swan

Section 3

Unsustainable trend 6:
development

Case-study 3.8

Conflicting national needs

Military developments proposed for the Northumberland National Park are an example of both a major development and incremental development. These add up to a significant change in the landscape of the Otterburn Training Area and raise questions about the commitment of Government departments to National Parks, which should be particularly strengthened by the UK Sustainable Development Strategy. Additionally, the 1995 Environment Act places a duty on departments to have regard to National Park purposes, a duty which conflicts with the Ministry of Defence's Otterburn proposals.

The 1996 proposals for training with the AS90 gun and the Multi-Launch Rocket System involve:

widening nearly 50 kms of existing road;

about 38 new and expanded gun spurs;

large lay-bys and tracks across the range;

and a 30,000 square metre central maintenance hardstanding.

There is also an array of other proposals which form part of a five year development plan. This plan was drawn up to try to address the problem of incremental development at the training area.

The physical developments add up to a major and lasting environmental impact, which undermines both of the National Park purposes. Yet this is only one part of the picture. There will also be a greater intensity of activity associated with this development, including the use of heavier weapons and those which cover long ranges. They will have impacts not only on the conservation of the Park but also on the opportunities available for people to enjoy it.

Should a National Park, specifically designated for conservation and public enjoyment, be the location for such developments? There is need for a public debate on the long term issues the proposals raise: sustainable development provides the right context as it gives equal weight to the environment and the needs of future generations with other interests.

Figure 8 Planning applications:
National Parks and neighbouring areas

Planning Authority	No. of planning decisions in 1995	Planning decisions per 1000 population
Brecon Beacons	**510**	**16**
Montgomeryshire	893	16
Cardiff	2 270	7
Broads Authority	**266**	**44**
South Norfolk	1 449	14
Norwich	969	8
Dartmoor	**600**	**19**
Caradon	1 190	15
Plymouth	1 297	5
Exmoor	**227**	**19**
Mid Devon	1 200	18
Taunton	1 380	14
Lake District	**978**	**23**
Eden	807	17
Preston	930	7
Northumberland	**57**	**14**
Tynedale	800	14
Gateshead	1 150	6
North York Moors	**573**	**22**
East Yorkshire	1 210	13
York	881	8
Peak Park	**891**	**21**
Macclesfield	1 842	12
Sheffield	2 497	5
Pembrokeshire	**499**	**22**
Ceredigion	1 301	19
Swansea	1 477	8
Snowdonia	**463**	**17**
Glyndwr	537	13
Colwyn	536	9
Yorkshire Dales	**609**	**32**
Teesdale	407	17
Darlington	746	7

December 1996

Source: Department of the Environment/ Welsh Office

Section 3

Unsustainable trend 7: threats to water quality and supply

Of particular concern to water quality and supply in National Parks are afforestation, degradation of peat moorland, nutrient enrichment and overgrazing. The Local Environment Agency Plans, developed by the Environment Agency, should address these issues.

Water: quality

Water pollution is becoming a significant factor in the degradation of the National Parks' environment, mainly from nutrient enrichment but also from incidents like the *Sea Empress* disaster off the Pembrokeshire Coast National Park.

Eutrophication of rivers and lakes – and the Broads – is a main concern of nature conservation strategies. Bassenthwaite Lake, a SSSI in the Lake District, is affected by eutrophication caused by sewage effluent. Eutrophication results in a loss of biodiversity and can cause problems for human users from toxic algae. Lake Bala in the Snowdonia National Park was affected by this in 1996, resulting in reduced access to the waterside.

The most dramatic example of pollution causing loss of wildlife is in the Broads, where inputs of phosphates from sewage treatment works are estimated to have increased tenfold since the beginning of the century. This has destroyed the ecosystem in some of the Broads and has led to the Broads Authority investing a significant proportion of its conservation budget on

Dredging the nutrient enriched mud at Barton Broad helps restore plant and animal life. Reducing run off from agricultural land and installing phosphate stripping plants at sewage works stops the problem recurring. Photo: Chris Swan

measures to clean up and restore the environmental health of the water bodies.

The impact of pollution incidents, like the *Sea Empress* disaster, could be mitigated if the National Park Authority had been able to take a co-ordinating role in the rescue operation and clean up. A report by Swansea University (Dyrynda 1996) suggests that more environmental damage was caused by the clean-up than by the spill itself. The Park Authority would have been able to focus clearly on the needs of conservation and recreation in the area. At present, decisions on matters affecting territorial waters below the low water mark rest with the Department of the Environment in conjunction with other departments. They can also grant licences for certain activities, thus acting in a landlord role as well. The right of passage of vessels in all territorial waters means that exclusion zones can only be made by international agreement on the grounds of safety, not ecology. **There is a need for the National Park Authority to be given a clear objective for conserving and enhancing the environment which embraces both coast and sea, which could include the possibility of establishing environmental exclusion zones.**

Water: supply

Demand for water affects most of the National Parks with very low water levels in reservoirs in dry periods, pressure for more abstraction from lakes and rivers and the threat of more reservoirs. Increased draw-down from natural lakes disturbs the ecology of the lakeshore and detracts from the natural beauty of the area. It also affects the ecology of rivers which drain the affected lake.

In evidence to the House of Commons Environment Committee Inquiry into Water Conservation and Supply, the Friends of the Lake District ask: "why must the golf courses in Manchester, the houses with large lawns in Cheshire, or the sports fields of Liverpool be kept verdant green during times of water supply stress whilst the Lake District and other high amenity areas suffer the draw-down effects ... or threats for the creation of additional damaging water impounding or water transfer schemes" (Friends of the Lake District 1996).

Water conservation is a key issue for water companies and companies that use water, as well as for domestic consumers.

Section 3

What do all these trends add up to?

In the following four pages the unsustainable trends have been projected onto a "virtual reality" National Park: Windy Moors. Computer technology enabled various components from typical National Park landscapes to be used to construct Windy Moors. Two farms are used as a basis for the land management of the area. Three possible futures for the Park in the year 2040, depending on how we act now, have also been constructed. The main changes are highlighted below but others will emerge from careful scrutiny of the images.

Windy Moors today

The typical National Park scene: with the business at Bottoms Farm (on the left) mainly depending on sheep farming. It has a small side line in tourism with a modest caravan site and its outbuildings are in need of repair. It has a hay meadow and receives support for managing this from the National Park Authority. It has a mixture of broadleaves and conifers on its land. Stone Quarry farm, on the right, is also a sheep-based business, with a newly built barn and a small stone quarry which has traditionally been used for local building stone.

The level of sheep grazing largely prevents any regeneration of natural vegetation, although there is some heather moorland.

Windy Moors 2040: business as usual

Bottoms Farm has given up sheep farming, plunging its resources into conifer afforestation, because of increasing demand in the British market for timber from "sustainably managed forests" and into the tourism business. Its outbuildings have developed into holiday cottages and it has more cottages on the old caravan site. It has sold its hay meadow to Water Enterprises plc for a reservoir, because of increasing demand for water. As water based leisure activities are now much more popular because of global warming, a car park has been built. The footpath to the water quickly became eroded and had to be surfaced with tarmac. Stone Quarry farm has sold its quarry interest to a big company dealing in aggregates and the quarry has expanded substantially. The need for lorries to transport the crushed rock and increased tourism traffic have led to the road across the hillside being straightened and widened. The Stone Quarry farm owners have a new pylon line across their land – this has been erected because of the demand for energy in the new developments surrounding the Park.

They have started arable farming – possible because of climate change and Government support for intensive production to meet increasing demand for food on a smaller area of land. The hillside is blackened because of increased fires from a hotter, drier climate and no heather remains. Telecommunications hardware is scattered across the scene.

Windy Moors 2040: most likely on current trends

This scenario assumes that Government policy on protecting National Parks has some impact and that several unsustainable trends are at least partially addressed. However the following seem inescapable: far more cars and straighter, faster roads; increasing demand for water leading to pressure for more reservoirs; sheep grazing pressure with very little semi-natural vegetation remaining; demand for energy related to increases in rural housing and other development; climate change in progress; demand for aggregates increasing.

Windy Moors 2040: a sustainable future

Bottoms and Stone Quarry farms are both thriving businesses, but their success is in harmony with the environment. Agricultural funding underpins this, providing incentives to reduce grazing levels and encourage conservation of hay meadows and other natural features. The management of native woodlands is encouraged and semi-natural vegetation is the dominant feature on the open hillsides. The buildings have been renovated using traditional materials from the local quarry. There are many visitors to this beautiful landscape, many brought by the post bus on the lane below Stone Quarry farm. Bottoms Farm operates a low key accommodation and refreshment business. Stone Quarry farm has a small telecentre for local people to use, enabling more working from home in a flexible way.

Which of these options is our legacy for future generations?

Section 3

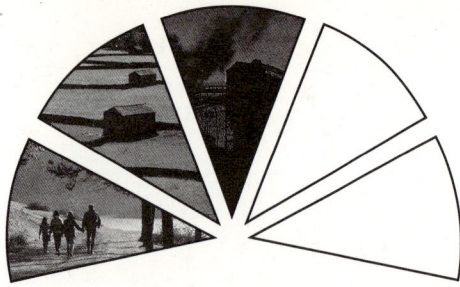

Section 3

Windy Moors today.

Windy Moors 2040: business as usual.

Windy Moors 2040: most likely on current trends.

Windy Moors 2040: a sustainable future.

Section 4: Who cares? People in the Parks

The environmental quality of National Parks is dependent on the nature of human interaction with them. This section particularly looks at those who live and work in them and at their relationship with the National Park Authorities and National Park Societies, which are the voluntary sector organisations working to uphold the National Park purposes in the individual Parks. It identifies opportunities and mechanisms for these groups to deliver the objectives of sustainable development, set out in the rest of this report.

National Park communities

People have lived in the areas now designated as National Parks for thousands of years. There are many differing views amongst today's National Park communities, both on the National Park designation itself and on what sustainability or sustainable development means in National Parks. The idea of environmental stewardship does seem to underlie many of the arguments, but there are differences over how the communities themselves should be sustained.

The Environment Act gives the National Park Authorities a duty to "foster the socio-economic well-being" of National Park communities, in pursuit of and taking full account of the conservation and enjoyment purposes. The Yorkshire Dales National Park Sustainability Appraisal (Baker Associates and Countrywise 1995) states: "the sustainability of the National Park, as a place, as a concept and as a designation, cannot be separated from, and indeed is dependent upon, the sustainability of its communities". But how are they to be sustained?

In the 1970s a public inquiry was held to determine an application for copper mining in the Snowdonia National Park. This brought into sharp focus the conflict between the agricultural way of life and mineral extraction. Meredith Roberts, a hill-farmer, told the inquiry:

"The financial gains from agriculture and afforestation no doubt look puny when compared with the wealth to be reaped by mining the copper ore ... but agriculture can last for ever if wisely practised and leaves the land richer in the end ... but the mining of an area only lasts until the ore-lode is exhausted ... after that the miner has no further interest in the place but moves on in search of the next minefield." (Searle, *cit.* Smith 1975)

Today there are lobby groups in some of the National Parks whose objective is to advance an economic argument, apparently at any cost to the environment. For instance, a group in Northumberland supports the Ministry of Defence application for the major development in the National Park on economic grounds (15 jobs would be created). The local economy and employment are a significant factor in many minerals applications. Ioan Bowen Rees, in Beyond National Parks (1995), argues that conservation arguments should not take precedence over the economic case "when nothing else palpable whatsoever is on offer". He advances the argument that the National Park designation presumes against the vitality of the rural economy, mainly by acting as a disincentive to development and investment.

This contrasts with Government advice (Department of the Environment circular 12/96)

Section 4

which says that there is no incompatibility between conserving National Parks and their remaining as living and working communities. It says: "the qualities for which the Parks have been designated are as much the products of man's hand as of nature. It is in the interests of the conservation of those qualities that the National Park Authorities have a duty to work with and for their local communities".

Socio-economic profile of National Park communities

In the light of these various arguments, establishing as accurate a picture as possible of the real socio-economic situation of the Park communities is essential. CNP has started the process by examining data from the National Office of Statistics on population age groups, size of population trends, the economic activity rate and the nature of employment.

Data basis

The National Office of Statistics (the Government's resource for population data gathered every ten years and more frequently in the case of employment data) provided "best fit" figures for National Park boundaries. Although there is generally a good level of correlation between the geographical basis for National Office of Statistics data and National Park boundary data provided by the National Park Authorities, some differences may occur. For instance, the total population figure provided by the NOS is 13.7% bigger than the figure contained in the Peak Park's 1991 Census Report (Peak Park 1995) because of the Park's fine-tuning around the boundary. The significance of these differences will be reduced when a global figure for all the Parks is used.

There is a need for National Park Authorities to work more closely with the National Office of Statistics to establish an agreed basis for data gathering for National Parks.

It should also be noted that where data from a previous Census are compared, boundary changes may have occurred which affect the comparison. However, as data are only available through the NOS, this has to be the basis for analysis.

The statistics supplied by the National Office of Statistics relating to employment are based on a 10% sample.

Comparison areas

The National Parks (NPs) data have been compared with relevant rural areas in England and Wales: the Rural Development Areas (RDAs) designated by the Rural Development Commission and the Mid Wales Rural Development Board (Mid Wales). The national average is also given where available, although this does, of course, include urban areas.

What the data show

Age groups:

Figure 9 suggests that National Parks have a significantly higher proportion of middle-aged population (45-64) than either other rural areas or the English and Welsh average of 19%. Perhaps surprisingly, Parks have a population over 60/65 which is more or less in line with the national average, and significantly lower than other rural areas. There is no evidence, therefore, that National Parks have a population tilted towards the over 60s at the expense of the young.

53

NATIONAL PARKS FOR LIFE: An agenda for action

Section 4

Figure 9 Age structure of National Park resident populations in 1991

Source: 1991 Census of Population

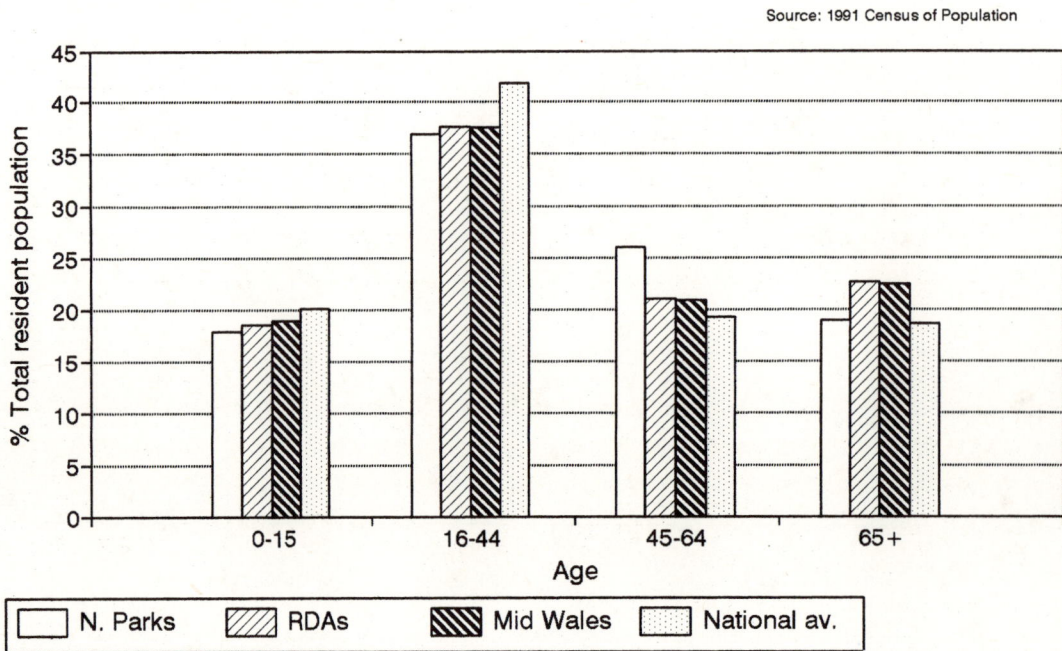

The population trend in National Parks over the last 40 years appears to have been upwards, following a dip in the early 70s (see figure 10). The Census figures for 1991 are compared with figures produced for a study on the economy of National Park communities (University of Edinburgh 1981) and with Countryside Commission figures. Rural depopulation appears to have been a trend over the last century until the 1970s and has been reversing since then.

Employment:

The data suggest that the percentage of the male population of working age which is economically active is 79%. Figure 11 shows a full breakdown of the figures for men between 16 and 64 for all the National Parks and compares the average with Rural Development Areas (77%), the mid-Wales Rural Development Board

area (76%) and with the national figure (75.5%). The female data are given in Appendix 2.

The figures suggest that the highest rates of economic inactivity for men in National Parks are Pembrokeshire (19%), Snowdonia (17%) and the Brecon Beacons (17.5%). These figures seem to reflect a generally higher level of male economic inactivity in rural Wales as a whole.

The employment structure of National Parks, perhaps not surprisingly, shows a great reliance on the tourism industry (which mainly falls under the distribution, hotels and catering heading but is also included under transport and other services). The "other services" category accounts for more than a quarter of jobs. This covers: school education, some parts of the civil service, medical and dental work and many visitor related activities (eg museums, tourist

Figure 10 National Park populations 1951 - 1991

Source: Census of Population 1951, 1971, 1981, 1991

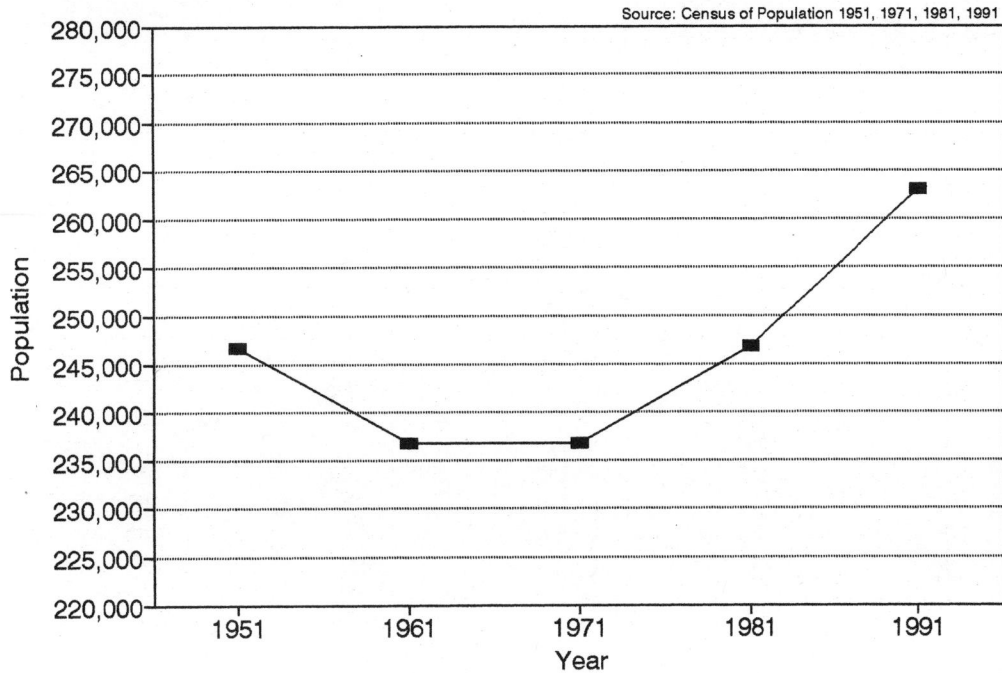

Figure 11 National Park male economic characteristics

	male population age 16-64	% male population age 16-64					
		economically active					economically inactive
		total employed	Employees		self employed	on a government scheme	Unemployed	
			F/T	P/T				
Park								
BB	9843	74.32	47.69	2.29	24.34	1.30	6.86	17.53
N	1359	82.78	50.33	1.40	31.05	1.69	3.90	11.63
D	9698	76.96	46.04	2.88	28.05	1.10	6.75	15.18
E	3541	79.78	35.67	3.36	40.75	1.07	6.86	12.28
LD	13687	83.57	51.34	2.76	29.47	0.77	3.45	12.21
NYM	8218	80.38	48.48	2.28	29.63	1.35	4.53	13.74
P	14267	82.23	52.66	2.33	27.24	0.64	4.30	12.83
PC	7423	70.58	40.24	2.09	28.25	1.56	8.64	19.22
S	8724	73.68	43.16	2.12	28.40	1.50	7.85	16.96
YD	6037	82.67	42.74	2.72	37.22	0.60	2.72	14.01
All Parks	82797	78.70	47.06	2.47	29.18	1.07	5.52	14.70
All RDAs	950730	76.63	53.88	2.14	20.61	1.36	7.84	14.17
Mid Wales	102773	75.79	45.89	2.24	27.66	1.45	6.56	16.17
GB	17392621	75.50	60.30	2.10	13.10	1.20	9.80	13.40

Compiled from 1991 Census of Population. Crown Copyright

Key: BB Brecon Beacons; N Northumberland; D Dartmoor; E Exmoor; LD Lake District; NYM North York Moor
P Peak; PC Pembrokeshire Coast; S Snowdonia; YD Yorkshire Dales; RDA Rural Development Area

Section 4

Figure 12 National Park employment
sectors (male and female)

Source: 1991 Census of Population

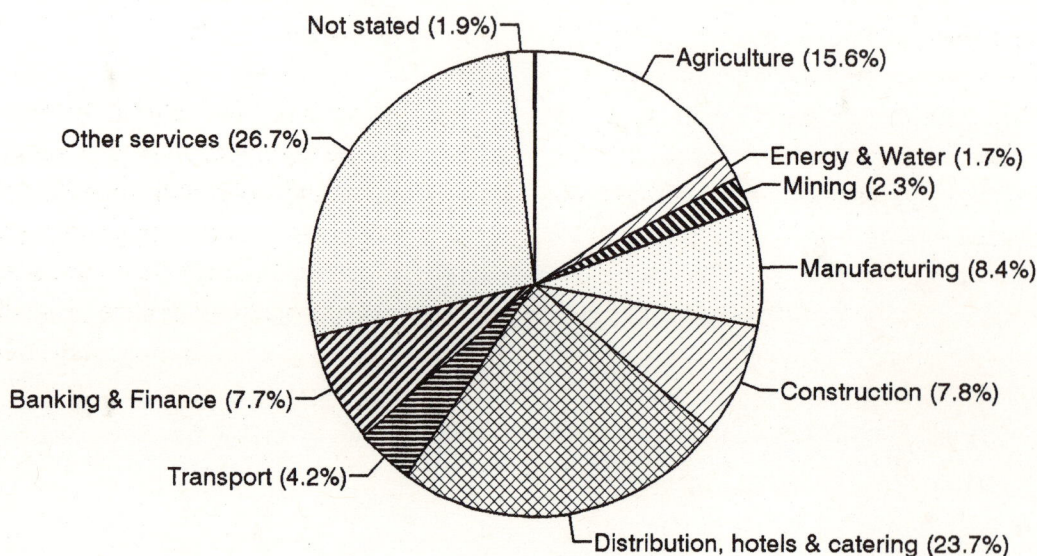

- Not stated (1.9%)
- Agriculture (15.6%)
- Other services (26.7%)
- Energy & Water (1.7%)
- Mining (2.3%)
- Manufacturing (8.4%)
- Construction (7.8%)
- Banking & Finance (7.7%)
- Transport (4.2%)
- Distribution, hotels & catering (23.7%)

offices, recreational services). Agriculture, forestry and fishing supplies one in six jobs (see figure 12).

The data show that the minerals extraction industry accounts for 2.3% of jobs (although some associated employment might fall under manufacturing and transport). It is more significant in some Parks than others (the data suggest 8% in the Peak Park compared with none in Exmoor). This compares with a 1981 figure of 14% provided by the Peak Park Board (Green Balance 1993) although this included people working in the Park but living outside it. The industry has recently become more mechanised and many hauliers are no longer employed by minerals companies but self-employed, so that their relationship to the industry is concealed in the figures.

Conclusion

The data discussed above suggests that more research is needed to enable the National Park Authorities to carry out their duties more effectively in relation to Park communities and to enable better protection for National Parks. There is no evidence from this data that the socio-economic position of people who live and work in National Parks compared to those in rural areas outside the Parks is such that it justifies permitting development that permanently damages the Parks.

Indeed the reliance on tourism, the service sector and agriculture suggests that protecting the environment of National Parks may be significant in protecting the socio-economic well-being of the Park communities. The

Section 4

Government guidance (Department of the Environment 12/96) recognises that the disadvantages of living in a National Park are geographical, including remoteness and climate (factors Parks have in common with their surrounding rural areas) rather than to do with the fact of designation. The guidance says Park Authorities provide significant benefits by being able to counter some of these factors: their visitor services support tourism and associated local purchasing and employment; they provide help to secure environmental land management funding and European Objective 5b funding.

Recommendations:

☀ **National Park Authorities should work more closely with the National Office of Statistics to establish an agreed geographical basis for data gathering for National Parks.**

☀ **The Council for National Parks will work for comprehensive sets of socio-economic data for the National Parks with meaningful comparisons (eg with surrounding rural areas) to be gathered. These should be publicly available and updated as new data become available.**

Section 4

National Park Authorities and Local Agenda 21

The 1990 Earth Summit produced an agenda for the 21st century, which set out how to address the challenges of sustainable development. It gave local authorities a central role in delivering this agenda of actions, which is known as Local Agenda 21. This process builds partnerships between local authorities and other sectors to develop and implement local policies for sustainable development. Central to it is "the ideal of actively involving the local community in working together towards sustainable development" (Local Government Management Board 1995). This involves:

awareness raising and education;

consulting and involving the public;

partnerships with groups within the local community;

measuring, monitoring and reporting on progress towards sustainability.

The LGMB also stresses the need for internal, green "housekeeping" and integrating sustainable development aims into policies and activities.

National Park Authorities have recently agreed a statement on National Parks, sustainability and work on Local Agenda 21. They see the statement as a "major contribution to the sustainable development of England and Wales and will involve National Parks in wider, regional, national and global debates on the best means of ensuring sustainability". This shift away from the traditional focus on sustainable land management is particularly welcome and is being implemented in various ways. The Snowdonia National Park Authority, for instance, is co-ordinating biodiversity action plans for its area in recognition of the inclusion of "wildlife" in the revised conservation purpose.

The statement makes a clear commitment to working with local people and making sure they all have an opportunity to participate in the Local Agenda 21 process. It also brings in a wider range of other partners including "private businesses and visitors, to reduce their adverse impacts on the environment and character of the Park". It says Park Authorities will work with "national government and agencies in pursuit of sustainable development". Getting across a message about National Park ideals is also a valuable objective in the statement. Once the principles are accepted by the individual Park Authorities and put into practice, this joint effort could put Park Authorities at the forefront of sustainable development and in delivering Local Agenda 21: an exciting start to the new era for the new National Park Authorities.

The following recommendations support the Park Authorities' intentions in taking a lead on Local Agenda 21:

– **National Park Authorities should fully exploit the opportunity that Local Agenda 21 provides for improving dialogue with local communities;**

– **National Park Authorities should initiate Local Agenda 21 processes that complement the work already being carried out by local authorities and which emphasise the qualities that make National Parks different from areas outside;**

– **Park Authorities should use the opportunity to work more closely with district and county councils and unitary authorities on sustainability issues;**

– **Park Authorities should make full use of the opportunity Local Agenda 21 provides for setting environmental targets and indicators that relate specifically to National Park purposes and values (see Section 2 on indicators);**

– **National Park Authorities should take a central role in co-ordinating biodiversity action plans for their areas;**

– **Park Authorities should use the Local Agenda 21 process to involve a far wider set of stakeholders and address a wider set of issues (including global issues) for the benefit of the conservation purpose;**

– **Park Authorities should exploit the opportunities provided by the revised second purpose for promoting understanding about National Park values to the corporate sector, National Park communities, neighbouring populations and government departments as well as visitors;**

– **themes for interpretation should focus more on National Park values and environmental messages, rather than being site based;**

– **Park Authorities should undertake audits of their own operations and set targets for environmental improvement.**

Tideswell 2000: Local Agenda 21 at work in the Peak

Summary

In 1995 the Peak Park Authority agreed to set up a Local Agenda 21 project in the National Park. This project is a partnership of county and district councils, the Rural Development Commission, East Midlands Electricity and North Derbyshire Health Authority and is one of several such projects across Derbyshire.

Tideswell is a village in the centre of the Park, with a population of 1,717. It was chosen in part because of successful community projects in the past and because the Town Council was keen to help develop a Local Agenda 21 (and is a member of the project Funding/Steering Group).

Youngsters in Tideswell planning their future. Photo: Peak National Park

The project was launched with an open day for all the village, which included a "planning for real" exercise – where people record problems, benefits and potential futures for their community. It was followed by a meeting with other sectors, like the health service, social services and youth workers. There proved to be some difficulty building Local Agenda 21 into their existing work programmes.

In early 1996 five local groups were set up looking at Local Agenda 21 from the perspectives of: young people, services in the community, buildings, local economy and employment and the environment. Feedback from these groups led to the formation of a Local Agenda 21 Forum which crystallised a draft agenda. The Forum organised an exhibition and publicity to share ideas with and get involvement from the wider village community.

Throughout, action in Tideswell has been facilitated by consultants contracted by the National Park Authority. The Park's Ranger and Education Services have been actively involved, in particular with the village school. The Local Agenda 21 Forum has been given a modest budget to encourage local initiatives and project ownership.

By kick-starting this Local Agenda 21 initiative, the Peak Park has demonstrated a key role for National Park Authorities in working towards Sustainable Development, although the cost (including in staff resources) is high. Funding is now being sought to allow Tideswell to take forward local action identified in the agenda. A couple of the first projects to start as a result are: updating the facilities at the youth club (but making sure it is done in an environmentally-friendly way) and looking into community composting.

Section 4

Sustainable rural emplo\tment

The National Parks Review Panel recognised the need to ensure the vitality of National Park communities, for the sake of the Parks themselves. Some National Park Authorities have been active in initiating or encouraging projects to support the local community whilst furthering the National Park purposes. There is clearly enormous scope for further work on this: for instance, by building stronger partnerships with the rural development agencies, which should in their turn recognise that any development in National Parks should further Park purposes. There is also scope for National Park Authorities to work more closely with companies and industries whose interests could help further Park purposes. Some examples are given in the case-study.

The 1995 Environment Act gives Park Authorities two complementary duties: in pursuing the purposes, to foster the socio-economic interests of Park communities and to take full account of the purposes. The guidance accompanying the Act (DoE 12/96) says that this should be carried out "in ways which are compatible with their pursuit of National Park purposes and with the need for appropriate economic development". Indeed the biggest sectors in National Park economies – tourism, agriculture and forestry – are potentially sustainable industries in the National Park context. How this might be achieved is discussed in the agendas in Section 5. National Park Authorities should be active in promoting opportunities for alternative employment where existing activities are not compatible with the Park purposes (for instance, where sectors of a community are dependent on minerals extraction as might be the case in some local areas of some National Parks).

There is a danger that the new duty may be interpreted in the narrow "economic" sense. However, Sustainable Development weighs social and environmental well-being equally besides economic need. Social well-being can be enhanced in other ways besides economic development: a good quality environment, for instance, is a significant contributor to our quality of life. National Park Authorities are in a good position to put sustainable development as the Earth Summit described it into action.

CNP recommends that:

– **all National Park Authorities publicise how they intend to implement their duty in the 1995 Environment Act to foster the economic well-being of National Park communities in pursuit of and taking full account of the Park purposes, including any successful initiatives already under way;**

– **any projects encouraged, promoted or supported by Park Authorities should have a comprehensive and inclusive approach to environmental management (including use of existing building and/or new building design; use of energy; draw on natural resources; transport policy; employment practices; open and accountable management approach; partnerships with environmental bodies etc);**

– **National Park Authorities ensure that the use of environmental assessment is promoted and that it includes alternatives to the development or project proposed;**

– **National Park Societies actively pursue better relationships with companies in order to secure a greater commitment to Park purposes and to encourage investment and employment to be compatible with sustainable development objectives.**

Section 4

What do microplants, silage wrap and teleworking have in common

Where National Park Authorities have encouraged alternative ways of working, the results have been very successful. There is enormous scope, especially in the light of the new socio-economic duty, for Park Authorities to act as a catalyst for encouraging economic activities which further the Park purposes.

The seven-year Integrated Rural Development Project in the Peak Park in the 1980s tried to do just that. It aimed to show: "how social, economic and environmental interests in rural areas can work together for mutual benefit" (Peak National Park 1990).

The project created 60 new full time jobs or their equivalent and helped many existing businesses improve their income. It also supported community schemes, including those which supported local traditions, like well dressing. Amongst new businesses to be set up were a high-tech microplants company using micropropagation techniques, a design award-winning cutlery factory and a tool hire business. In 1993 the project was awarded a top countryside conservation prize by the Royal Institution of Chartered Surveyors.

Beacons Country Products is an EC funded initiative of the Brecon Beacons National Park Authority. It aims to improve the economic viability of farms and their surrounding communities, whilst safeguarding the environment for future generations. It involves enterprises like the Farm Film Producers Group, which collects and recycles black plastic silage wrap and work with the timber co-operative Coed Cymru on producing and processing timber in ways that are compatible with sustainable development.

Sometimes, identifying potentially beneficial new technologies can provide opportunities for sustainable development in the Parks. The Rural White Paper (Department of the Environment/MAFF 1996) draws attention to the opportunities now available to rural communities and businesses by the telecommunications and information technology revolution.

There are now about 150 telecottages in the UK, eight of them in four National Parks. A televillage is being built in the Brecon Beacons National Park and the Eccles House telebusiness centre in the Peak Park provides jobs and training for local people. A project in the Yorkshire Dales National Park, Dalesnet, aims to connect and co-ordinate information technology systems and develop new ones for the benefit of communities in the Dales. Although the environmental benefits need to be carefully weighed against any impacts, teleworking has the potential to influence positively a new era of employment in National Parks.

The Farm Film Producers Group: community involvement in a recycling project. Photo: Brecon Beacons National Park Authority

Section 5: A full repairing lease: what we can all do

"Future generations will have inventions which we cannot even dream of, but with our help they will also have the National Parks that we know and love", Brian Redhead, CNP Past President.

Section 3 painted a grim picture of National Parks in 2040. This section looks at the positive trends: what all the relevant interest groups are and should be doing to ensure the Parks of the mid 21st century are even better than today. It tracks the key players from the international community to National Park communities. It then identifies the key issues which need tackling for sustainability to become operational in the National Park context and makes recommendations for the relevant key players.

IUCN

The World Conservation Union (IUCN), through its Parks for Life process of consultation and final report, drew up an action plan for Protected Areas. It called on international bodies, governments and government agencies plus non-governmental and community organisations to help make a reality of the plan. This report attempts to do that in some part. Its themes are echoed here: "community involvement, the need to plan and manage protected areas in their wider context, and the importance of seizing opportunities as well as responding to threats" (IUCN 1994).

European Community

The European Union's Fifth Environmental Action Programme has the theme of "Towards Sustainability". This takes up the sustainable development theme, "whereby the root causes of environmental degradation are addressed before the problems become so pressing that they can no longer be ignored". It targets "behavioural patterns of producers and consumers, governments and citizens".

The EC provides funding for pilot projects and promotes models of production to demonstrate what is possible. These include the LIFE financial instrument and the cohesion fund for less-developed regions of the Community to achieve development goals while ensuring environmental protection. However there is a need for all EC Structure Funds to have environmental underpinning.

The United Nations Environment and Development UK Committee

This body follows up the commitments made at the Rio Summit in the UK. It involves statutory and voluntary organisations. Its key priorities are energy conservation and stimulating environmentally friendly products and practice. Whilst district and county councils have a high profile on it, National Park Authorities do not. In 1997 the Rio process will be reviewed by the United Nations Commission on Sustainable Development and the work of the UNED-UK Committee will feed into that.

The Government

At a national level there is now a battery of documents supporting the objectives of sustainable development and enhancement of biodiversity. National Parks and the opportunities

for sustainable development that exist within them provide a chance for the government to implement some of these policies.

This report has three messages for Government:

Message 1: New duty

All Government departments should demonstrate clearly how they are implementing their new duty to have regard to the Park purposes.

This does not mean leaving it up the Department of Environment. The challenge now is for the effective integration of environmental stewardship – which includes defending the National Park purposes – across all Government departments. This is particularly true for the Treasury, when it comes to priorities for spending and the funding of National Park Authorities, the Welsh Office, the Agriculture departments, the Ministry of Defence, the Department of Transport and the Department of Trade and Industry. Integration of environmental concerns, particularly into the agriculture and tourism sectors, is a priority for the EU 5th Environmental Action Programmes, mentioned above.

Message 2: Resources

Maintaining an adequate level of funding to National Park Authorities, as the National Parks Review Panel recommended, is a cost effective way of delivering sustainable development. In order to deliver their contribution to Sustainable Development objectives National Parks need adequate funding.

In 1991 the National Parks Review Panel recommended that a one-third increase in National Park spending was needed to secure its recommendations. It said that this sum could be contained within an overall increase of 10% in real terms, spread over four or five years. It said: "in our view, this is a fairly modest price, even at a time when public expenditure of all kinds is under close scrutiny, to secure the best of our landscape heritage". The level of funding announced at the end of 1996 goes some way to addressing this and should mark a new era of Government commitment for adequately funded, free standing Park Authorities.

Message 3: New Parks

The designation of new National Parks, notably the New Forest and South Downs, is a pressing need in the light of sustainability objectives on biodiversity, tourism and the conservation of lowland landscapes.

The south of England is under great pressure from development and from recreational demands, yet two key areas which are crucial to wildlife conservation, which meet the landscape criteria for National Park designation and which are heavily visited remain outside the National Parks family. Designation of the New Forest and South Downs would contribute to national strategies for managing leisure activities, as they are so close to major areas of population and would enable better protection of these areas by placing National Park values at the centre of management strategies.

The Statutory Agencies

The revised National Park purposes in the 1995 Environment Act provide an opportunity for a much stronger partnership on National Parks between the Countryside Commission and Countryside Council for Wales, the traditional

defenders of National Parks, and other bodies like English Nature, English Heritage and CADW (the heritage agency in Wales). This not only brings more players to the table but enables a better understanding of the different perspectives and cultures of the organisations, within the focus of specific geographical areas. The potential benefits for National Parks are enormous, allowing for a more integrated approach to sustainable development across a range of disciplines. Whilst English Nature has actively welcomed and acted on the new first purpose for National Parks, much work remains to be done by the heritage agencies.

National Park Authorities

The setting up of new, free-standing National Park Authorities under the 1995 Environment Act is the start of a new era for National Parks. It provides an opportunity for setting a new agenda for National Parks which will ensure their sustainable use for the next 50 years.

National Park Authorities have traditionally focused their attentions on land management issues. National Park Management Plans are a good medium for allowing a dialogue between differing audiences and putting sustainable land management into practice.

Turning to less land management focused areas is now a vital way of achieving core objectives and would be a welcome change of emphasis. Often, some of the trends which have the most serious implications for environmental sustainability of National Parks originate outside the Parks or are questions of social behaviour. National Park Authorities have enormous opportunities to influence public behaviour, not only in their relationships with National Park residents and visitors but also with corporate interests whose activities affect the Parks.

Environmental voluntary organisations

There are three objectives for this report in relation to environmental voluntary organisations:

- to encourage National Park focused organisations to become more involved in the sustainability agenda;

- to encourage organisations with a sustainability bias to become more focused on the contribution National Parks make to that agenda;

- to encourage stronger partnerships between National Park Authorities, Societies and local groups of national organisations (like Friends of the Earth, the Worldwide Fund for Nature, the Council for the Protection of Rural England or the British Trust for Conservation Volunteers).

The Council for National Parks has some 40 member conservation and amenity organisations, including the eleven National Park Societies. Some of the member organisations – notably the Council for the Protection of Rural England, the Campaign for the Protection of Rural Wales, the Royal Society for the Protection of Birds and the National Trust – have been key players in the debates at national level on sustainability and biodiversity. However this is not a theme that has been widely adopted by others, particularly the National Park Societies whose National Park level of influence is particularly valuable. Local Agenda 21 provides a vehicle for achieving sustainability objectives and is a way of working more effectively in partnership with others, like the National Park Authorities and local communities.

There are also many environmental organisations – like Friends of the Earth, Greenpeace and the Worldwide Fund for Nature – which have been particularly active on sustainability issues. Yet they do not always include a National Park dimension, despite the importance of National Parks to issues like climate change and enhancement of biodiversity. This means that renewable energy technologies have been promoted even where they could cause lasting damage to the landscape of National Parks. And opportunities to use Parks as testbeds for sustainable development or to promote their experience and achievements, particularly in sustainable land management, have been overlooked. Such organisations often have local groups, which include highly motivated individuals and a tradition of experience in many aspects of environmental work.

Companies

The impact of corporate sector activities is discussed more fully in the companion report, "Not Ours but Ours to Look After". Companies' activities affect National Parks in many ways: when they operate in the Parks; when they consume Park products; when their remote emissions or transport routes affect the Parks; when they target National Parks for best practice or for testing environmentally friendly technologies.

The Corporate Forum for National Parks was set up for companies which recognise the unique value of National Parks and want to demonstrate their commitment to them. The Forum has worked closely with CNP in developing the agenda for companies.

The objective is for companies to establish a corporate commitment to National Parks at board level. This involves a menu of action:

1. Establish, at board level, a corporate commitment to the unique value for conservation and quiet recreation of the National Parks of England and Wales and to their local rural character.

2. Incorporate this into, and implement it through, any environmental management system, environmental management and audit system (EMAS) or any other system for auditing and environmental reporting.

3. Inform employees of this commitment.

4. Publicise this commitment in annual reports and/or environmental reports.

5. Inform customers of the commitment to National Parks as part of a green marketing strategy.

6. Ensure the corporate commitment to National Parks informs an environmentally responsible purchasing policy.

7. Assess the company's plans, policies, location and/or activities in relation to National Parks, taking the following into account:

i) the National Park purposes to conserve and enhance the natural beauty, wildlife and cultural heritage and to promote opportunities for understanding and enjoyment of the special qualities of National Parks by the public;

ii) the Environment Act 1995's duty on organisations and companies defined as "statutory undertakers" to have regard to the National Park purposes in their activities affecting the Parks;

iii) planning policy guidance note 7, which states that a proposal for a major development in a National Park should be assessed in terms of the national need for the development and whether any alternatives exist.

8. Set targets for reducing any negative impacts on the National Parks.

9. Set targets for positive performance enhancement in National Parks or which benefit National Parks directly or indirectly.

10. Prioritise National Parks for any environmental improvement or investment where a whole company strategy is not possible.

National Park communities

The 1995 Environment Act revised the membership of the National Park Authorities to include a greater level of parish/community council representation. This provides a good opportunity for National Park communities to become more involved with the work of the Authorities and particularly to be able to focus more clearly on the Park purposes. Some National Park communities have felt alienated from the decisions of the Park Authorities. Local Agenda 21 is another useful mechanism for more closely involving communities and for allowing communities to develop initiatives of their own in moving towards sustainable development.

Consumers

We are all consumers of National Parks, whether we live in them, visit them or never do either. Urban lifestyles draw heavily on the natural resources of National Parks, including water, minerals, the products of agriculture or forestry. Yet the connections are rarely made and the impacts hardly perceived. The Agendas that follow identify lifestyle and other changes that would really benefit National Parks and the whole environment.

Section 5

The Agendas

The following issue-based agendas attempt to make the connections between National Parks and modern living. How can we, at the end of the twentieth century, make sure that our lifestyles not only meet our needs for the means of survival and a good quality of life but also do not compromise the ability of our grandchildren to meet theirs? National Parks present an opportunity for positive action. The actions recommended below all aim to support the vision of National Parks in 2040:

Beautiful landscapes where: water, soil and air are pure natural landforms are preserved wildlife flourishes a range of distinctive cultures is expressed in the built heritage and the everyday lives of Park residents livelihoods derive from activities that the environment can sustain erosion of the special qualities would not be contemplated unless society could find no other possible solution everyone can find a source of spiritual renewal and opportunities for quiet enjoyment we can all gain a greater understanding of the whole environment and of National Park values

Buttermere in the Lake District – we can all help to protect such places by following the agendas. Photo: Ian Brodie

Agenda on energy

There are three key areas for action where benefits lie for the long term sustainability of National Parks: energy conservation (by far the most important area) including improving energy efficiency; renewable energy; overhead lines.

Energy conservation

Reducing the demand for energy and using energy more efficiently are top priorities within sustainable development strategies. The benefits for National Parks would be related to global trends as well as to local impacts:

– reduction in the impact of climate change;

– reduced acidification in already sensitive areas;

– reduced need for energy infrastructure (pylons, wires, sub-stations, gas pipelines, wind turbines, HEP, tidal barrages etc);

– less need for Flue-Gas Desulphurisation which, although National Parks are avoided as a source, puts pressure on Parks to supply limestone for other uses.

It involves making connections between urban lifestyles and the special environment of National Parks. The best way forward is for Parks to act as models of good practice. Two examples are given in the case-studies.

Renewable energy

There are some conflicts between renewable technologies and National Park designation, as discussed elsewhere. These range from landscape impact to ecological and other changes, including the loss of rivers allowed to follow their natural courses. However, there is a place in National Parks for small-scale schemes where there is a nationally determined need which cannot be met in any other way and where it can be demonstrated that the environmental benefits, taking into account the need to further Park purposes, have been clearly established. For example, Exmoor National Park Authority has acquired an old, water-powered sawmill and wants to restore it, using the surplus energy to supply local homes.

Overhead lines

There is also the specific issue of power lines which compromise the natural beauty of National Parks. The quality of the landscape is inextricably a part of the sustainable development debate although some

companies and Government have given it a lower priority compared with other considerations, like chemical pollution. Landscape quality is an important consideration for the energy (and indeed tele-communications) companies which are "statutory undertakers" with a duty under the 1995 Environment Act to "have regard to" National Park purposes in "exercising or performing any functions in relation to, or so as to affect, land in a National Park".

As a result of power station location and the way in which the energy industry has developed historically, National Parks appear to be locked into the supply system even where it would be desirable by today's environmental standards to change the pattern of supply. This is a complex issue, where many barriers exist to action. The following recommendations are based on discussions at a roundtable involving environmental organisations, the countryside agencies, OFFER (the electricity industry regulator) and companies on the issue of energy and telecommunications transmission lines in National Parks.

– the domestic energy levy of £1 per customer for energy conservation, which is administered by the Energy Saving Trust, should be extended beyond the 1998 cut-off date;

– improvements to existing networks should include: undergrounding; rerouting; redesign; new development to a high standard which furthers Park purposes where possible; phasing in new locations for generation to avoid the need for sensitive trans-Park routes;

– opportunities for undergrounding should be explored when line refurbishment is being planned;

– memoranda of agreement should be drawn up with various sectors establishing a code of practice in relation to National Parks;

– National Park Authorities should involve all utilities in drawing up National Park management plans;

– as part of this process companies' policies could be included in the management plans and the National Park Authority's policies could be cross-referenced into companies' plans;

– it is important for National Park Authorities and the voluntary sector to identify the different timescales for decision making in different companies and to feed in to the process at appropriate opportunities;

– the scope for sharing facilities should be explored – this process could be facilitated by the countryside agencies;

– the Department of Trade and Industry should initiate a process of strategic environmental assessment of the energy industry to provide the context for considering the many complex issues;

– independent research should be carried out into the relative costs/benefits (including to the environment) of undergrounding and the scope for it within the existing network – at present the industry is the only source of information. This could be initiated by the countryside agencies;

– work on geographically focused enhancement initiatives would be useful (and could be promoted as success stories). This activity could be based on partnerships between National Park Authorities and Public Energy Suppliers: real success has been demonstrated where a rolling programme of partnership projects has been initiated, indicating a willingness to co-operate and share costs.

General recommendations for key players

These centre on two themes: trying to reduce greenhouse gas emissions which lead to climate change, and planning to manage the climate changes already forecast to occur over the next 50 years.

National Park Authorities should consider initiating energy conservation and management strategies for the whole of the Park area. These could be undertaken in partnership with district councils which have a statutory duty in relation to energy conservation. These would be designed to address greenhouse gas and acid emissions and the issues raised by energy infrastructure. The strategy would represent a coherent plan for reducing demand for energy and assessing the impact, in the National Park context, of energy supply. It should also make connections between the sources of energy supply (eg power stations outside the Parks) and areas supplied within the Park, plus energy transmission lines that cross National Parks.

Strategies should include internal, domestic, agricultural and tourism energy users, plus any other major industrial energy users in the area.

Voluntary sector organisations should work with the Energy Saving Trust and their public energy supply company for the establishment of local energy advice centres, where none exists at present. National Park Authorities should consider adding their support.

The new second purpose for National Parks includes promoting opportunities for understanding the area. **National Park Authorities and voluntary sector organisations** are well placed to disseminate an energy conservation message to visitors and Park communities which would have general and specific benefits.

For instance, energy saving should provide a more dominant theme in **National Park Authority** information centres, where there is a unique opportunity to make the links between National Parks and lifestyles.

Companies have a valuable role to play by reducing demand for energy. This is discussed in detail in the report for companies "Not Ours but Ours to Look After."

All these strategies for energy conservation harmonise with the Government's action plan to limit climate change, notably:

"renewed efforts to improve energy efficiency; improve minimum energy efficiency standards for domestic appliances and office equipment" (Department of the Environment news release 1996).

Planning to manage change

Despite the difficulty of predicting the outcomes of climate change, experts suggest that managers of protected areas should start planning now to manage the changes ahead. **National Park Authorities** should now enter a phase of contingency planning for dealing with climate change. This should involve a wide set of partners: "the importance in all countries of private land managers to the long-term survival of the protected area system cannot be stressed enough" (Bridgewater 1996). This planning involves areas outside the network of designated areas and therefore requires a strategic overview.

These individual strategies should be supported by research initiated by **the Department of the Environment** and the **Welsh Office** on the possible effects of climate change on National Parks. This will enable the National Park Authorities to plan ahead and manage for climate change. The work carried out by English Nature and the Broads Authority is a good model. This research would apply and update the work of the Countryside Commission on the potential impacts of atmospheric pollution on the English countryside and should also include Wales. The work would focus specifically on National Parks because of the partnership with National Park Authorities, where environmental management is a primary function. It would produce many lessons with a wider relevance.

The Council for National Parks, the Park Authorities and the countryside agencies should lobby for this research on climate change to be carried out and should involve other environmental organisations.

Case-study 4.2

Saving energy helps National Parks

CNP Scheme

The Council for National Parks has promoted a model energy conservation scheme targeted at National Park residents, which can be taken up by regional electricity companies. CNP developed the scheme in partnership with the Energy Saving Trust, and Northern Electric has piloted the project.

The scheme involves a package of half price energy saving measures, like loft insulation and hot water tank jackets. It is being offered to National Park residents with electrically heated homes.

The scheme is intended to address concerns about climate change, acid rain and the issue of pylons in beautiful areas. It also has the potential to spread an environmental message in an area of high environmental quality.

The costs of the discounted package are met by a levy on domestic energy bills. The Energy Saving Trust oversees this budget which led to £20 million of investment in energy saving measures between 1993 and 1995. The work of the Trust aims to meet Government targets on energy saving and emissions of greenhouse gases.

Snowdonia audit

The Snowdonia National Park Authority commissioned a feasibility study on promoting practical implementation of energy conservation in the Park.

This concluded (Dulas 1996) that an energy conservation project should be set up. This would reduce energy by at least 10% a year in the target sectors, reduce carbon emissions significantly and yield possible savings of over £1 million per year to householders and businesses.

The study recommended that the scheme should target the domestic, commercial and transport sectors, in particular: home-owning households, serviced accommodation, static caravan sites, schools, National Park Authority buildings and traffic management schemes. The scheme could include an energy audit and proposed that an energy advice centre should be set up, as none exists in north Wales.

The report includes a lengthy section on traditional and innovative energy conservation techniques, targeted at specific sectors.

CNP President, Sir Chris Bonington, fits a low energy light bulb at his home in the Lake District. Photo: Chris Swan

Section 5

Agenda on land management

Sustainable land management in National Parks does not just have the objective of sustaining food production, the livelihoods of local communities, biodiversity and primary resources but also of conserving and enhancing the natural beauty of the landscape and the cultural heritage of the area. It must achieve all this against the background of the Common Agricultural Policy support for production and the particular challenge of managing marginal, upland areas. The task involves many partners: farmers and landowners, from big companies to traditional small businesses to the National Trust; National Park Authorities; the Agriculture departments; the Forestry Commission; the countryside agencies and so on. It is a dynamic process which does not aim to fossilise a countryside of a bygone era but to make sustainability operational in a specific geographical and legislative context.

The following set of recommendations should be seen in the widest context: that of making agriculture more sustainable across the whole countryside. A report by the Council for the Protection of Rural England and the Worldwide Fund for Nature identifies seven measures that would help achieve this: "a lower and more discriminating use of inorganic fertilisers; improved management of farm wastes; a more discriminating approach to pest control; enhanced protection of water resources; reduction in agriculture's contribution to air pollution; appropriate stocking and grazing patterns and the protection, management and enhancement of farmland habitats and landscape features" (CPRE/WWF 1996).

In National Parks there are already some good working models, which display some of these features, from which the whole countryside would benefit. The Rural White Paper (DoE 1996) said these kind of approaches in the Parks "can now be applied throughout our countryside ... we need to build on the achievements of the past 50 years by finding new ways to enrich the quality of the wider countryside". However nowhere is there a comprehensive scheme which brings in landscape and wildlife enhancement, air, water and soil quality.

The MacEwens (1980) recommended "a new support system that could guarantee the future of hill farming and the achievement of the wider purposes of the national parks". The recommendations below build on all these ideas:

Agricultural support

A straightforward, integrated environmental land management package should be available which is robust, attractive, voluntary, simple to use and reliant upon compliance with any legal responsibilities (this would replace the multiplicity of countryside schemes – ESAs, six agri-environmental schemes, Countryside Stewardship in England, Tir Cymen in Wales and National Park farm schemes).

The package would comprise an integrated suite of different components because separated blocks of funding may be easier to protect from cuts.

The scheme should have application across the whole countryside and requires fundamental reform of agricultural support. Although this is a matter for **Europe and Government**, National Park Authorities should promote model schemes, building on their existing farm schemes. Demonstrating that such schemes work is a vital basis for lobbying by the **Association of National Park Authorities and the voluntary sector.**

The scheme would offer a menu of environmental goods which farmers and landowners could offer to safeguard or produce. These would include hay meadows, unimproved/semi-improved pastures and wet grasslands. There would also be support for producing more beneficial products (eg functional features that will be valued in the future, like dry stone walls and barns). The scheme would thus combine buying more environmental products with buying good management.

National Park Authorities should take a lead role in delivering the scheme in their areas, administering resources on behalf of the relevant Government departments, which should retain their budget responsibilities. This would build on the small beginnings already made: the Snowdonia National Park Authority's partnership with the Countryside Council for Wales on Tir Cymen and the delivery of Countryside Stewardship in the North York Moors, Northumberland, Peak District and Yorkshire Dales.

The basis of the scheme should be whole farm plans which would involve all the components of an agri-business: production; pollution prevention; ecological sustainability; recreation; visual and other amenity. No publicly funded options would be environmentally damaging.

The scheme would replace the system of headage subsidies for livestock production with an area-based system reflecting the environmental, economic and social role of livestock production. This would require changes to EU policy and CNP supports lobbying to secure these changes.

Section 5

Agenda on land
management

The Council for National Parks will lobby with others for such a scheme to be made available, adequately funded and delivered locally.

In the absence of an integrated scheme:

– the whole area of all the National Parks should be eligible for an agri-environment scheme, which would combine the best from the current range of schemes such as ESAs, Countryside Stewardship, Wildlife Enhancement, Habitat Scheme, Moorland Scheme, National Park farm schemes;

– National Park Authorities should be given the opportunity to deliver the existing schemes in the Parks and to work with other agencies, on an integrated basis to encourage better take-up, reduce confusion and maximise environmental benefits;

– National Park budgets should be maintained and enhanced to enable this work to be carried out;

– Process: all applicants for any agri-environment schemes should be guided to National Park Authorities, thus maximising the opportunity to encourage applicants towards sustainable environmental land management. This already happens in the Snowdonia National Park. This would be of value to applicants by reducing bureaucracy, making advice on the range of options easier to obtain and permitting more tailoring of options to local circumstances. National Park Authorities should be able to advise the relevant Government agency on applications and endorse applications for national schemes.

In all cases the national Government agencies should continue to provide the funding.

Blaen y Glyn farm at Llanfachreth: two generations of the Ashton family still work on this award winning farm. Photo: Chris Swan

Section 5

Land management case-study

Tir Cymen in the Snowdonia National Park

The Tir Cymen scheme set up by the Countryside Council for Wales and administered in Meirionnydd by the Snowdonia National Park Authority is generally hailed as a resounding success. Both environmental organisations and those representing farmers and landowners have called for the scheme to be extended throughout Wales and to be used as a model scheme for England too. Its key feature is that it maintains and enhances the natural beauty of the landscape and wildlife habitats, whilst sustaining rural incomes and jobs.

Tir Cymen involves voluntary participation on a whole-farm basis, with ten year agreements drawn up. The scheme rewards farmers for environmental work, including capital projects such as hedge laying and dry stone wall restoration, and prescriptions like not using fertiliser on unimproved grassland and heather management. At the same time it maintains farming jobs and generates new employment. It is estimated that about 100 new jobs have been created in Meirionnydd alone. Part of its success in Snowdonia rests on the involvement of National Park Authority staff who act as field officers for the scheme. They are uniquely placed to work with the farming community in a way that is sensitive to local agronomic conditions, local farming culture and National Park values.

A recent survey for the Countryside Council for Wales (CCW 1996) found the scheme helped boost the average farm income by £3,400 a year in Meirionnydd and helped 29 out of 35 local businesses generate new demand for their services in the three pilot areas. There were demonstrable benefits for landscape maintenance and enhancement and for wildlife.

Ty Coch farm at Ffestiniog: dry stone wall building is a major job creator. Photo: Chris Swan

Section 5

Agenda on land management: forestry

The following principles should underpin sustainable forestry policies within National Parks (ie, sustainable in terms of National Park purposes including landscape, wildlife, cultural heritage, public amenity and impacts on air, soil and water quality) with the aim of providing a more varied woodland mix through natural regeneration of appropriate tree species where possible:

– there should be a vision for particular areas and objectives agreed for beneficial change: these should include the total removal of forestry as an option as well as adding new areas of native woodland or managing existing woodland better;

– options should be subject to environmental assessment of all the impacts: including landscape, ecological and recreational;

– Strategic Environmental Assessment of forestry operations on a national scale should be carried out and would provide a valuable context;

– planting and management strategies should be drawn up, which give a high priority to enhancing landscape and wildlife quality and to promoting quiet enjoyment. Planting strategies should emphasise species composition and design;

– Clear felling should be avoided unless there are clear conservation gains, with the objective of maintaining a continuous vegetation cover and seeking to sustain a more varied woodland mix of appropriate tree species – emphasis should be on pocket or selective felling and a design-led approach;

– least damaging technology should be used in felling exercises;

– targets should be agreed for increasing the area of native woodland in every National Park: the Native Woodlands Accord negotiated between the Park Authorities and the Forestry Commission and local memoranda for action, based on the national accord, represent helpful progress;

– moorland planting should not be ruled out if it meets landscape and biodiversity enhancement criteria. Neither should the removal of forestry from some areas for the same reasons. However, either of these should only be carried out as part of a landscape vision for the National Park, which establishes an appropriate balance for different kinds of habitat;

– there should be a full exploration of the potential for creating wilder areas where natural processes play a greater part in determining the vegetation;

– it should be recognised that sustainable management of existing woodlands is crucial;

– on farm or on site environmentally benign processing should be carried out where possible to add value to National Park forestry products and to enable farmers/owners to have a greater financial incentive for management;

– locally grown and sustainably managed timber should be used for National Park Authority purposes (as in Exmoor and Pembrokeshire).

The mobile double slabber used by Coed Cymru in the Brecon Beacons National Park adds value to sustainably produced timber products by on-site processing. Photo: Brecon Beacons National Park Authority

Section 5

Agenda on land management: partnerships

National Park Authorities should involve a wider range of private sector/land ownership interests in the formulation of policies, plans, objectives, targets and delivery mechanisms. This will help win hearts and minds and encourage shared visions, not just shared policies!

One way of doing this would be to set up a liaison group bringing all interest groups together on a Park by Park basis. This would complement the work being carried out by MAFF's Regional Agri-Environment Consultation Groups. The group would decide how best to apply schemes to achieve Park objectives and act as a joint lobbying body for reform. The group should include not just economic interests but others with a stake in land management issues, for instance visitors and non-farming communities.

The National Park Authorities should work with major landowners to establish what it means to further National Park purposes. This involves putting greater effort into helping land managers understand the features, wildlife and recreational values of their area and will enable better delivery of environmental services.

The English and Welsh agriculture departments should consider seconding staff to work within National Park Authorities as part of establishing more effective delivery mechanisms for environmental farming support.

Influencing consumer behaviour

Consumers are becoming increasingly concerned about the present system of agriculture. There is not only concern about possible links between agricultural practices and human health but also awareness of the impacts on the general state of the environment, including the quality of the landscape. Many consumers are keen to see examples of environmentally-sensitive practices in action but have limited choices in how they can support a better system.

Consumers pay for agricultural production both through taxation at the production end and out of net income at the retail outlet. They should be confident that they are buying a safe and sustainable agricultural system as well as an ample supply and diversity of products. In achieving this the links between agricultural support, agricultural practices, the environment and the products that are available must be made clear.

National Parks are a good focus for changing consumer behaviour and raising awareness of these complex issues.

How can this be done?

1. Get National Parks into the market place

National Parks are associated by the public with high environmental quality. Their agricultural products, where they are environmentally-sensitively produced, should be identified and promoted as such. An example might be sheep products from farms where environmentally sustainable grazing levels are achieved. Products from farms which are part of a National Park farm scheme would be another. Considerations could also include animal welfare and the use of pesticides. National Park Authorities, in partnership with food quality experts, could set out the criteria and establish an accreditation system. The Park Authority should retain control over the accreditation but could arrange for another body to administer it. Each National Park could start by having one distinctive product which it intends to promote in this way. The accreditation should meet recognised environmental standards from the outset so that it cannot be the subject of accusations of false and exaggerated "green" claims. It should also be based on a cradle-to-grave assessment of products, including any planning aspects, to ensure all parts of the production process are sensitive to the National Park environment. The accreditation needs to command the same respect as the Soil Association symbol.

Supermarkets should be targeted for the promotion, capitalising on regional purchasing policies where they exist. "Mass buying power has transformed British farming, and critics blame the supermarket buyers for the disappearance of traditional products and many small growers, as well as a concentration on uniform appearance rather than taste and texture" (Guardian 13/4/96). National Parks are a good basis on which to start changing this relatively recent trend.

The big supermarket chains should be lobbied to put more effort into promoting product distribution which allows for regional distinctiveness, reduces the need for road transportation and extends the range of sustainably produced products thus allowing more consumer choice. At present many chains promote general product diversity at the expense of local product diversity.

Lambs grazed on salt marshes in Brittany are promoted as a premium product – lambs are produced in the same way in Wales but not promoted as such. Derbyshire supermarkets stock pitta bread

Section 5

Agenda on land
management: partnerships

but not local oatcakes. Why is it possible to buy a full range of French regional cheese in some supermarkets, but not English or Welsh ones? Promoting a range of National Park cheeses could prove to be an attractive marketing device.

National Park Authorities with expertise in land management and good liaison with farmers and producers are uniquely placed to start such initiatives. The Brecon Beacons Park Authority has made an important start by operating a mobile slaughter hall in the National Park – the first to be licensed. This aims to reduce the impacts of transportation on livestock and provide consumers with a quality produce whose origins can be traced back to source. Supermarket chains should be encouraged to promote such products and price them attractively.

Far more work needs to be done before such a scheme, with potentially great benefits for sustainable development, could get off the ground. **The countryside agencies, the National Park Authorities and the agriculture departments should consider working together to initiate further research with the objective of launching a pilot scheme in the medium term.** The new duty for public bodies to have regard to Park purposes and the socio-economic duty of National Park Authorities in the 1995 Environment Act provide the legislative impetus.

2. Raise public awareness

The accreditation strategy should be supported by a public awareness campaign from the voluntary sector and/or via National Park Authority visitor centres and interpretation programmes. Big supermarket chains should be encouraged to market the products in a high profile way, making clear the links between beautiful landscapes, a high quality environment and good food.

3. Develop the product range

National Park Authorities could work with farmers and producers to add value to products (eg, by more local processing) and to add to the range of products. An environmental product development strategy would benefit National Park purposes and help foster the socio-economic interests of the Park communities. It would build on the achievements of the National Park farm schemes and demonstrate in a more visible way that National Parks are indeed role models for the whole countryside.

The Council for National Parks is grateful to the following organisations and individuals for advice and/or participation in a land management seminar. Their ideas have helped inform this section and the section on intensive agriculture:

Association of National Park Authorities; British Mountaineering Council; Country Landowners' Association; Countryside Commission; Countryside Council for Wales; Forestry Authority; National Farmers' Union; National Trust; North West Water; Northumberland National Park Authority; Northumberland Wildlife Trust; Peak National Park Authority; Royal Society for the Protection of Birds; Rachel Thomas; Roger Williams.

Section 5

Agenda on minerals

Government policy, consumer behaviour, higher standards in the minerals industry, and a firm stand by National Park Authorities all have a part to play in making the supply of minerals – and particularly aggregates – more sustainable. As David Pearce wrote in Blueprint 3: "Any coherent policy on aggregates would have to connect demand reduction, recycling, planning betterment and pricing in a highly sophisticated manner: not easy" (Pearce 1993).

The following principles should underpin a coherent set of policies for the more sustainable use of the natural mineral resource in National Parks. The objective is to ensure that, within a context of reduced demand for minerals, the only minerals being supplied from National Parks meet a national need and are without alternatives, which is far from the case at present. This means taking full account of existing consents when considering new proposals. Any operations in Parks should be of the highest standard.

Policy principles and Government Action

– reduce the demand for minerals (the Government's cuts in the road building programme have made a contribution here, but it is likely to be short-lived);

– promote better husbandry and the efficient use of the primary mineral resource;

– give priority to using secondary and recycled aggregates over primary materials where possible;

– use the least environmentally sensitive sources of supply: the Department of the Environment should undertake a strategic environmental assessment of minerals resources which would provide a framework for minerals planning.

– introduce a primary aggregates tax – this would help value the resource more appropriately and "build in" the environmental cost of using it. A premium rate of tax on aggregates supplied from National Parks and Areas of Outstanding Natural Beauty would reflect the Government policy on supply of minerals from those areas.

– address the key issues of aggregates forecasting and landbanks, which are based on meeting an unsustainable level of hypothetical demand;

– ensure that specifications are the minimum possible consistent with safety and longevity requirements.

The benefits of a primary aggregates tax are that a proportion of it could be allocated to fund restoration in National Parks where there is no possibility of requiring the relevant owner to do this, in order to break the cycle of "extensions for landscaping", to buy out the most sensitive dormant permissions and to provide alternative, sustainable employment opportunities for those directly reliant on the minerals industry. This proposal would have the following effects:

– introduce part of the environmental cost of minerals extraction into construction programmes and projects;

– help reduce demand;

– help encourage research and development of alternatives and ways of reducing demand;

– promote the use of secondary aggregates;

– provide a level playing field for companies seeking to improve their environmental performance;

– enable targeted funding of environmental improvements to address the legacy of past permissions;

– support strategies for Sustainable Development set out by the Government.

As a first step **the Department of the Environment** should initiate its long-promised research project on how a taxation system could be applied to primary aggregates.

The Government should work with minerals suppliers and consumers to work out optimum specification levels, to address the safety issue and to secure an adequate supply and quality of secondary materials.

Action by Park Authorities

Extensions to existing permissions

Applications for extensions to existing permissions in National Parks are part of a trend which is maintaining the pressure on National Parks to provide an unsustainable level of aggregates for many generations. There is a growing tendency by companies, too often accepted by National Park Authorities, to emphasise the potential for reshaping the landscape in order to justify such applications and on the short term gain of jobs.

When it comes to mineral working, incremental permissions of this kind undermine the first purpose of National Parks: to conserve and enhance the natural beauty of the landscape. In line with Government policy such applications should not be allowed save in exceptional circumstances. That means assessing the national need for the mineral and whether there are

Section 5

alternative sites or alternative ways of meeting the need. The scope for restoration should only be assessed once those criteria are met.

The public inquiry into the application to extend working at Spaunton Quarry in the North York Moors provides an opportunity for this. The developer did not attempt to justify the application on grounds of national need: "there was no case of overriding need for the mineral which would justify the granting of consent" (Mineral Planning June 1996). National Park Authority members overturned a recommendation for rejection by officers. The call-in by the Secretary of State will enable the arguments to be tested at a more strategic level.

Last bite agreements

National Park Authorities should ensure that last bite agreements (which bind companies to cease work completely by a certain date) are drawn up and that they really are binding. A Section 106 agreement with an end date to working does not have the same effect. Companies with end dates to working naturally plan to continue beyond that if viable reserves still exist.

Only a legally binding agreement sends out the right signal and allows companies to plan ahead with clear ground rules. Such an agreement has been made at Swinden Quarry in the Yorkshire Dales, where the developer is to sell the land to a conservation body once restoration is complete.

End uses

National Park Authorities should seek to ensure that no mineral leaves a National Park quarry without a specified end use. This would enable trends to be monitored, limit quarrying in National Parks to minerals which require a Park location and allow wise use of precious resources in the sort of timescale sustainable development requires us to consider.

Action by Local Authorities

Local Authorities have a part to play in achieving the best use of minerals. **Controlling end uses through purchasing policies and through planning conditions and policies is a key means of doing this.** They should also integrate minerals and other policies more, eg, by specifying the maximum use of primary materials in maintenance contracts.

Action by Consumers

Consumers of minerals can adopt a policy of avoiding National Parks as sources of minerals where they can. Companies can, for instance, ensure that the only minerals used from National Parks meet a national need and are without alternative. The policy of avoiding National Parks as a source of supply has already been adopted by some companies, including National Power in relation to limestone for flue-gas desulphurisation.

The Council for National Parks will continue to work to raise consumer awareness about the environmental problems associated with the level and sources of supply. It will make the necessary links – for instance between paper production and the use of china clay from National Parks.

The Minerals Industry

The minerals industry is increasingly active on issues relating to sustainable development: wise resource use is a policy objective many minerals companies embrace. Wise resource use in National Parks means only extracting minerals in them when no alternatives exist and when high grade or special specifications are required. Within the terms of sustainable development, future generations need National Parks as much as they will need minerals, and using resources wisely means taking that into account.

The following would help advance the policy objective of wise use of minerals:

Minerals companies should make a corporate commitment to National Parks, recognising their unique importance for conservation and quiet recreation.

This commitment can be implemented as follows:

– pledge never to seek to open any new site for minerals working in any National Park unless the particular mineral required meets a national need and cannot be supplied from any other source;

– a first step would be to consider National Parks as a last resort, considering all other alternative locations first;

– pledge to relinquish any site with dormant planning permission for minerals extraction in a National Park (volunteer not to oppose a Prohibition Order): this goes further than the present position that they should not be re-opened without the imposition of modern planning conditions;

– do not seek to extend an existing site for minerals extraction unless the particular mineral required meets a national need and cannot be supplied from any other source;

– publicise the commitment and any measures taken to implement it as part of a corporate environmental promotion strategy;

Section 5

– lobby throughout the industry to persuade other companies to follow suit. This would lead to the creation of a level playing field so that environmental responsibility is not penalised in a competitive market.

Also:

– ensure that any mineral supplied from a National Park only just meets the specification required, rather than far surpasses it;

– plan the end state of a site at the earliest possible opportunity in consultation with the National Park Authority;

– minimise environmental impacts during the working life of the site.

The industry should also investigate more closely the scope for increasing the range of technically suitable alternative supplies by:

– using lower specification deposits, by themselves or blended with other materials;

– upgrading deposits with a higher proportion of waste materials so that these can meet requirements normally satisfied by purer deposits that require less processing;

– working deposits with larger quantities of over-burden.

The industry should investigate both generally and at specific sites the alternative uses for lower quality aggregates such as scalpings and dust which are produced as by-products of the excavation and preparation of higher grade materials. This should include the scope for processing scalpings to graded material to increase the proportion of quarry output that meets higher specifications.

Joint actions

There is more scope for research by the Government and industry, including architects and designers, on:

– designing structures and construction materials so that they can be more efficiently recycled at some future date;

– designing resource-lean structures and materials;

– use of waste materials. In some cases this may mean using higher quality, but longer lasting, minerals.

These arguments are set out more fully in the companion report for companies, "Not Ours, But Ours to Look After".

Section 5

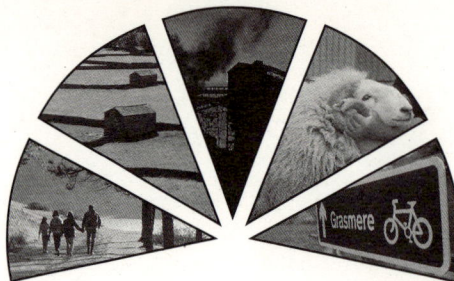

Agenda on transport

The burden of road transport on National Parks is so heavy that any strategies to relieve it are immensely valuable. However, Park level strategies are difficult to make effective without national policy backing. This would mean **an integrated national transport strategy, involving a strategic environmental assessment which would take into account legislation and Government policy on National Parks.**

In the case of National Parks there is a strong link between visits made to the Parks and the impact of private car use. Of the 76 million visits made annually, 91% are by car (Countryside Commission 1996a). The sustainability appraisal for the Yorkshire Dales National Park Authority stated: "it is hard to reconcile any large generator of private car trips, be it a shopping centre, theme park, or area of natural beauty, with the principles of sustainability" (Baker Associates and Countrywise 1995). The House of Commons Environment Committee report on the Environmental Impact of Leisure Activities identified an urgent need for "rural transport strategies" for managing leisure use of the countryside (House of Commons 1995).

A policy objective for National Parks on transport therefore is **to reduce the dependency of residents and visitors on cars.**

Targets must be set to support this and strategies drawn up to implement it. The Royal Commission on Environmental Pollution has set a target reducing the current 95% proportion of leisure journeys made by car to 80% by the year 2005 (RCEP 1994). The Yorkshire Dales National Park has set a target of stabilizing traffic flows at 1994 levels (Traffic and Visitor Management Strategy 1996). Any such targets have to recognise the fact that car use at a high level will continue for the foreseeable future as long as individuals retain the choice and present incentives to use a car.

Target-setting for reduction of car use contrasts sharply with the policies set out in the Rural White Paper, which places heavy emphasis on road transport and particularly the use of the private car. Maintaining the road network is its priority. It does however acknowledge that the projected increases for leisure traffic will have "unacceptable consequences in many areas" (DoE/MAFF 1995).

Countryside Agencies

The Countryside Commission has put forward proposals for charging cars to drive in National Parks (there are numerous ideas from National Parks in other countries that could be examined) and for a 50 mph speed limit on rural roads, and is discussing these with the Government.

The Countryside Council for Wales' document "Transport and rural Wales" (CCW 1996a) encourages people to visit the countryside without using a car. It bases its policies on public transport integrated with the needs of walkers and cyclists.

National Park Authorities

Traffic management

The Government has lent its support to traffic management strategies for all National Parks. Some Park Authorities have taken a lead on this and given support to public transport, although others have done little. The Peak Park has been one of the leaders, piloting road closure schemes and the provision of alternative forms of transport. It secured a big Department of Transport grant for public transport and traffic calming measures in the Hope and Upper Derwent Valleys carried out in 1996. The Department of the Environment's guidance on National Parks (DoE circular 12/96) very helpfully encourages Park Authorities to work with local highway and traffic authorities to develop appropriate schemes for traffic and transport management in consultation with local interests.

The Dartmoor traffic management initiative and investment by some Park Authorities in public transport are highlighted in the case-study and one of the recommendations that follows draws on the lessons to be learnt from these experiences.

A partnership project for the North York Moors National Park on traffic management (Oxford Centre for Tourism and Leisure Studies 1996) looked at several options, including inverse charging for car parking (where charges are high to begin with, then reduce to encourage people to leave their cars in one spot) linked to a public transport system; developing model consultation and consensus-building procedures (public meetings were not a good consultation strategy for traffic management proposals); rurally-based park-and-ride schemes; selected toll roads within Parks. But all these would need further research before all the benefits and impacts could be identified.

Traffic management is also visitor management (see next agenda): "If you restrict or limit parking you reduce erosion of nearby footpaths. If you develop new cycling and walking routes in more robust areas ...

Section 5

this will also take pressure away from damaged areas. If you provide public transport to enable everyone, not just car drivers, to reach the National Park, you will avoid over-concentration of circular trails from car parks. And if you use skilful education and marketing techniques ... to create awareness of alternative places to go to, and alternative ways to travel, then you will reduce many of the negative impacts" (Speakman 1996).

The 1995 Environment Act provides a mechanism by which National Park Authorities can and should start weaning people from their cars. The Act puts into practice the Sandford principle, so that Park Authorities should make every effort to reconcile any conflicts which may arise between the two purposes. The methods described by the circular accompanying the guidance would be helpful in addressing the problems of leisure car use: "mediation, negotiation and co-operation". The Act also says that in cases where an irreconcilable conflict exists the conservation purpose takes precedence: a principle that could be applied to management of leisure traffic.

Public Transport

CNP recommends that National Park Authorities, in partnership with local authorities, should have a duty, the powers and the resources to provide recreational public transport services in the Parks using the most environmentally efficient technologies available. Money spent on public transport should be viewed as an investment rather than a subsidy, and Government and local authority funding to National Park Authorities should recognise this. Any vehicles used should be of an appropriate scale for the road system in the Parks.

Encouraging public transport would have the welcome benefit of enabling more people without access to a car to visit the Parks. All the National Parks have gone some way on supporting public transport. A key way of encouraging more people to use it is by providing information about services and integrating it with information on walking or cycling. The Lake District National Park Authority's 1996 publication was a good example of what can be achieved. National Park Authorities should also encourage inter-ticketing between transport modes, a family fare rate and promote public transport as an attraction in itself. *Countrygoer* magazine, produced by Transport for Leisure, provides up-dates on the latest National Park initiatives. **Park Authorities and Park Societies** could do more to encourage rail companies to improve services which access Parks and to integrate them with other modes of transport.

Consumers

Influencing consumer behaviour when it comes to car use is notoriously difficult. The Royal Commission on Environmental Pollution's report on Transport and the Environment said that the success of greener lifestyles depends "on the action taken by central and local government to provide frameworks within which individual choices can be exercised in an environmentally responsible way".

Targeting the tourist industry to reduce car based activities is one way forward. This means encouraging businesses not to promote visits or activities that are car dependent, to make better use of public transport (and lobby for improvements to services), to promote the use of alternative means of transport (including walking) and to provide services that reduce dependence on cars.

CNP will also encourage publishers of guide books not to promote the kind of visits or activities that are car dependent. It would be very helpful for each National Park to have its own showpiece scheme which gets across the message that leaving the car behind can be fun. Visitors to Exmoor are not convinced by hearing about alternatives to car use in the Peak Park! Personal experience is the best persuader and small first steps are immensely important.

The **National Park Authority** information centre is a natural focal point for getting across environmental messages. Reducing car use, supported by provision of alternative means of transport like cycle route development, would make a strong theme. The Yorkshire Dales Park Authority has carried out a sustainability appraisal of its walks, talks and events programme.

The **National Park Societies** also have a part to play by not organising activities which are car dependent and campaigning to reduce car use. This could involve a car park campaign, where car based visitors are made aware of the impacts of car use and guided to attractive – and fun! – alternatives.

Voluntary organisations should adopt policies in support of public transport in National Parks. Only too often members of environmental organisations blame the "common tourist", and not themselves, for car congestion despoiling a beautiful environment. The British Mountaineering Club's magazine has debated the issues raised by the Lake District Traffic Management Strategy (BMC Summit – issue 2 1996). As one member writes: "we are part of the problem and part of the solution."

Traffic growth projections imply such serious impacts on National Parks and other rural areas that action is required on many different fronts by the different actors set out above in the short term.

Section 5

Transport case-study

National car parks?

Summary

Securing local support for traffic management strategies in National Parks is not always easy, but making public transport work is a success story in many Parks.

The Dartmoor National Park Authority traffic management strategy was approved in 1994 following extensive public consultation. This included a study of the Plymouth-Burrator corridor and included a survey to determine patterns of use around Burrator Reservoir. This was to address concern about heavy car use at the site leading to congestion and conflict with other road users. Proposals included road closures and traffic calming in Dousland.

The study was supported by a Department of Transport grant and consultation involved public exhibitions and a public meeting. The proposals were subject to many objections. A report to the Park Committee (June 1996) states: "the intended advantages of a car free environment, better recreation opportunities and better access by bus and bicycle were not perceived by most respondents as being real advantages ... the volume and hostility of the opposition came as a complete surprise".

The Park Authority now feels it cannot proceed with the Burrator proposals, except elements of it that are supported. However its overall traffic management strategy remains in place: "based upon the principle of sustainability and the belief that reducing the dominance of the car will, in the right circumstances, bring benefits both locally and globally".

The Lake District Traffic Management Strategy has also suffered from organised opposition, including from the Cumbria Tourist Board, although there is no evidence that properly designed traffic management schemes mitigate against business interests.

One way of addressing this problem may be to adopt consensus-building techniques along the Agenda 21 model (see Section 4).

This suggested process would involve earlier consultation, starting with a blank sheet of paper; ensuring all key stakeholders are invited to share a common vision which would include raising awareness of National Park purposes, identifying problems and then producing solutions; working with smaller groups, not public meetings, and publicising the results to break down any potential public alienation; working to implement solutions identified then moving towards the next phase. This is clearly a longer process and more resource intensive but may secure lasting and better supported results in the long run. There would be value in setting up small-scale pilot schemes to demonstrate what can be achieved.

Another way is to provide real alternatives to car users. In 1996, demand was so high for the North York Moors National Park Moorsbus that duplicate services had to be operated. 48% of users had access to a car but chose the Moorsbus because of its relative cheapness, frequency, reliability and good promotion. The Sherpa bus in Snowdonia provides access to the busiest parts of the Parks, stops on request and allows walkers to climb Snowdon by one path and descend by another.

Section 5

Agenda on recreation

National Parks were designated in part because of the opportunities they provide for enjoyment, and providing opportunities for enjoyment is one of the statutory purposes of Park Authorities – so recreation is part of their *raison d'àtre.* As part of the sustainability debate there has been a growing emphasis on visitors' numbers, with an assertion that numbers of visitors to National Parks are environmentally unsustainable. The reasons often cited are footpath erosion (particularly on long distance trails) and visitor density at popular sites. The House of Commons Environment Committee's report on the Environmental Impact of Leisure Activities found no evidence to support the view that visitor numbers were causing lasting ecological damage.

What is Green Tourism?

A report looking at sustainable tourism in Europe's National Parks (FNNPE 1993) defined it as: "all forms of tourism development, management and activity, which maintain the environmental, social and economic integrity and well-being of natural, built and cultural resources in perpetuity".

This supports the view that it is not visitor numbers as such that are unsustainable. It is rather the nature of the visit that is potentially unsustainable: particularly the means of transport used and the nature of activities.

National Parks were designated for everyone to enjoy, not a select few, but they are not all things to all comers. **The opportunities for understanding and quiet enjoyment that they provide should be treated as a distinctive contribution to regional and national recreational strategies.**

Making facilities available for the enjoyment of the countryside – and promoting them – outside National Parks is part of a strategy for sustainable management of leisure activities nationwide.

As the previous section identified, private car use is the most unsustainable aspect of most visits made to National Parks. Tackling this must be a priority for action. Footpath erosion is far more of a problem on routes from car parks than on most long distance trails (some of which are on inherently unsustainable terrain), although clearly management and restoration of long distance trails can be resource-intensive.

The features of sustainable visitor management for National Parks are:

– the availability of public transport or safe and enjoyable routes where muscle power can be used;

– making visitors aware of the problem issues for heavily visited sites, so they do not add to the problem, and making non-vehicular access to them readily available and convenient;

– promoting the long walk-in where appropriate, eg by moving car parks further away from paths to mountain summits;

– maintenance and restoration of heavily visited sites, eroded areas or public rights of way;

– ensuring that visits respect and complement the cultural heritage of the area;

– engaging visitors in direct conservation work or securing indirect support for it;

– involvement of the local community and its skills in visitor management.

Upholding the principle of quiet enjoyment in National Parks is part of sustainable visitor management. Noisy, motorised sports are unsustainable in the National Park context because they may conflict with the first, conservation purpose and may prevent others from taking advantage of opportunities for quiet enjoyment and understanding. Such activities may change the expectations of what the National Park experience is and therefore compromise the ability of future generations to enjoy the tranquillity available to us today.

The Sports Council should be encouraged to agree a memorandum of agreement with the Association of National Park Authorities on what constitute sustainable sporting activities in National Parks. This would complement the various codes of practice that have been agreed by different sporting bodies.

Green Tourism

Some **National Park Authorities** are promoting green tourism, often in partnership with others, to ensure that the demand for recreation does not conflict with the need for conservation. The Peak Tourism Partnership was a three year pilot scheme. It involved the relevant statutory agencies, plus the National Park Authority, the English Tourist Board, the regional tourist boards and companies including Center Parcs and Severn Trent Water.

It drew up visitor management plans for honeypot sites, identified mechanisms for raising money from visitors for environmental projects and emphasised interpretation as a means of visitor management. It also identified transport as a key issue and worked on

Section 5

public transport initiatives.

The South Devon Green Tourism Initiative, covering the Dartmoor National Park, came up with a Green Audit Kit that tourism businesses could use. This provided practical information on a variety of issues. Both of these projects are described in "Sustainable Rural Tourism" (Countryside Commission 1995).

Stronger partnerships between **National Park Authorities and/or the Association of National Park Authorities and voluntary organisations** with national marketing capabilities for conservation holidays (eg the British Trust for Conservation Volunteers, the Ramblers' Association or the National Trust) could be fruitful.

Tourism businesses operating in National Parks should be encouraged to act in a more sustainable way by:

– reducing demand for energy;

– introducing better waste management (including minimising waste and recycling);

– supporting the local economy by using employees, products and services from the locality and by supporting traditional skills and economic activities;

– offering a discount to those arriving by public transport;

– providing information about walking/cycling/public transport;

– directing people away from honeypot sites or activities by providing information about alternatives;

– promoting activities which are not car-dependent;

– raising clients' awareness of National Park purposes;

– supporting practical conservation work in the Park.

Development Proposals

A discussion paper by CNP on tourism complexes (CNP 1988) highlighted real problems from large scale timeshare/leisure developments, and favoured "small scale, low key tourism". It concluded: "If large leisure complexes are allowed to develop in the Parks at the expense of the unspoiled, uncommercialised qualities of the Parks, it is the small businesses that will suffer most and that will suffer first". There is a real danger that revival in the economy could bring a flurry of new applications for major tourist developments in the Parks, as at the end of the 80s. As CNP's Past President, the late Brian Redhead warned: *"The National Parks are leisure centres in themselves. They are to be enjoyed for themselves. They do not require vulgar adornments. They are not development sites".*

The Government and regional tourism boards should acknowledge that large scale tourism development directly conflicts with the Park purposes, undermining both conservation and opportunities for quiet enjoyment. Companies considering new development in National Parks should consider:

– is the development is really necessary?

– will it protect and enhance the Park?

– will it offer an opportunity for quiet enjoyment?

– will it fit into the landscape and be on the right scale?

– will it be in tune with the character of the Park?

– will it enhance the cultural heritage of the area?

– will it fit into the local economy?

– will it bring lasting benefits to the Park's environment, residents and visitors?

– is there scope for bringing a sensitive new use to an existing building?

Section 5

Agenda on Planning and Development

Many planning issues have been covered in other sections, but there are key points about the planning system itself, where sustainability issues arise. The National Parks Review Panel concluded that: "National Parks represent a national capital asset. Developments that damage their special qualities involve the expenditure of that asset. We may lack the vocabulary and the conceptual framework to quantify that expenditure, but that does not mean a significant loss has not taken place, or that the nation is not poorer for it" (Edwards 1991).

Sustainability is not about stopping all development but ensuring that the right development takes place in the right place at the right time. The right framework for planning in National Parks is vital in achieving this.

Legislative and policy context

Development Plans (which set out the main considerations on which planning applications are decided)

The 1995 Environment Act set up a mechanism for most National Park Authorities to become structure plan authorities (this means they can set out key, strategic policies as a framework for local planning) – the welcome implementation of one of the key National Parks Review Panel recommendations. The new system will provide an excellent opportunity for National Park Authorities, backed up by effective partnerships and consultation, to develop effective systems for putting sustainable planning at the strategic level into action.

Because of the clearer focus that the new Authorities will have on the National Park purposes the new planning remit enables National Parks to act as role models for sustainable development. The Government should support the decisions taken where they contribute to the objectives of sustainable development (see the Peak Park case-study on page 60). The principles of the development plans should clearly focus on the National Park purposes and the contribution Parks make to sustainable development objectives. **The countryside agencies should continue to monitor and advise on the development plans for National Parks.**

Major development test

National Parks are subject to a test for major development set out in Planning Policy Guidance Note 7. This states that such development should not be allowed save in exceptional circumstances and should be rigorously assessed according to a set of criteria, including whether it meets a national need and whether there are alternative locations or alternative ways of meeting the need.

This test is also set out in the Government's White Paper, "This Common Inheritance" (UK Government 1990): "Major industrial or commercial development will not normally be permitted in National Parks: only where there are proven national needs and a lack of alternative sites can any exception be justified".

Planning Policy Guidance Note 1 sets out a framework for the planning system to achieve sustainable development. This specifically recognises that designated areas of national landscape importance should be safeguarded.

Minerals Planning Guidance Note 1, in its objectives for sustainable development for minerals planning, includes: "to protect areas of designated landscape or nature conservation value from development, other than in exceptional circumstances and where it has been demonstrated that development is in the public interest" (Department of the Environment 1996a).

Despite this recognition of the importance of National Parks there is evidence that damaging major development has and continues to take place in National Parks.

CNP believes that the Government would enable more effective implementation of its principles of sustainable development set out in the UK Strategy if the test for major development in National Parks were to be revised to remove the loopholes that deflect attention from the issue of national need, and to ensure that it covers all forms of major development proposals.

The new test should state that:

"Proposals for major development in National Parks should not take place save in exceptional circumstances. Applications must be subject to rigorous public examination, and it is must be demonstrated that they satisfy the following conditions:-

i) that the proposal is absolutely necessary in the national interest, which includes the furtherance of Park purposes;

ii) that the proposal cannot practicably be accommodated in an alternative location outside the National Parks

In determining whether a proposal is absolutely

Section 5

necessary in the national interest full regard shall be had to -

i) the prospects of meeting the demand which gives rise to the need for the proposal by means other than the proposal;

and

ii) the prospects and means of reducing the demands which gives rise to the need for the proposal.

Any proposal satisfying these conditions shall only be permitted subject to conditions which mitigate so far as practicable any adverse environmental effects including the submission of a restoration plan for when the need for the development ceases".

This proposed test makes no reference to the impact on the local economy (as do PPG7 and MPG6), instead returning to the first principles that other Government policy sets out. At present the local economy is often used as an overriding reason to permit damaging development. The benefits to other sectors of the local economy in not proceeding with a damaging development are never included in the rigorous assessment required for major development proposals, as they could be. Therefore, CNP believes that, for clarity, the test should focus on the need for a development and whether alternatives exist.

Development control

The Council for National Parks monitors planning applications across the Parks to identify potentially damaging proposals or trends. The Countryside Commission has taken a decision not to monitor applications at this level. It will only intervene if asked to do so by a Park Authority or if an issue of exceptional national significance emerges. CNP feels this decision is potentially dangerous for the future sustainability of the Parks. Many unsustainable trends only emerge by rigorous monitoring of individual applications. **CNP will continue to make this important task a priority and urges the Countryside Commission to reconsider its decision.**

A new planning test

The legislative and policy context for planning and development in National Parks is strong. Yet the evidence is still of a heavy pressure for development which is not sustainable.

To address this CNP believes that all National Park development plans should include the following policy considerations for assessing all applications. Any proposed development in a National Park should:

1. serve and/or enhance the National Park purposes;

2. represent an appropriate way of serving the purposes.

For reasons of practical implementation, it would be up to the discretion of individual National Park Officers to decide if applications were of so little significance that they would not need to be assessed in this way.

National Park Plans

The Environment Act 1995 gave the new National Park Authorities a duty to consult widely in drawing up non-statutory management plans. These cover a much wider area than development, including water catchment and other forms of land management. **The process for drawing up these plans represents a good opportunity to consult with a wider range of partners, including private sector companies. Policies of such partners should be included in the plans, with the opportunity for reciprocation offered.**

Environmental Assessment

Planning Policy Guidance Note 7 states that a higher proportion of applications in National Parks should be subject to environmental assessment than elsewhere. This is consistent with European policy because of the potentially significant impact of major developments on National Park purposes.

Park Authorities may ask for any environmental assessment to include a rigorous assessment of alternatives to the development. This option is not generally carried out at present. Park Authorities should take the necessary steps to satisfy themselves that alternative means and alternative locations have been rigorously assessed when considering major development proposals. The Department of Environment should consider whether Park Authorities could be enabled to carry out this work themselves and pass on the cost to the developer, if this is not undertaken with sufficient rigour in the environmental assessment.

Consultation

Planning and development control is the area in which local communities are most likely to enter into conflicts with local and National Park Authorities. Improving consultation is a vital tool in securing support for environmentally-led policies. The "Planning for Real" exercise in the Brecon Beacons National Park is a good example. In the light of pressures to speed up the development plan process, this should be viewed as a rolling programme of consultation, rather than being tied to the formal plan timetable.

Planning case-study

Planning for Real in the Brecon Beacons

In 1992 the Brecon Beacons National Park Authority, against a background of poor and sometimes hostile public opinion, had to draw up its first Park-wide local plan. "We needed to find some way of getting to the heart of the complaints, to disperse the confrontational atmosphere, to encourage consensus and involve the communities in the decision making process" (Brecon Beacons Park Authority information sheet).

The Park Authority decided to adopt "planning for real" techniques – which aim to involve local communities at a much earlier stage of planning than normal. They are presented with maps or models of their area and asked to make decisions about its future.

The Brecon Beacons project involved 39 meetings covering all the communities in the Park. Rather than taking a "them and us" approach the Authority described the events as "a structured jumble sale". Old style consultation tends to attract middle-class articulate people. The new approach involved a far wider cross-section, from hill farmers to young people.

The Authority concludes that the "public relations benefit has been enormous, writing the Local Plan has been more thorough with the issues there to focus attention".

The process is resource and staff intensive. It involved two planners and one assistant full-time for a year plus a part-time community development officer.

The real test of the process lies in the future and will be measured by the nature of relations between the Park Authority and local communities and the level of support of those communities for the National Park purposes. If either of these is enhanced, the process will have contributed significantly to the achievement of sustainability objectives.

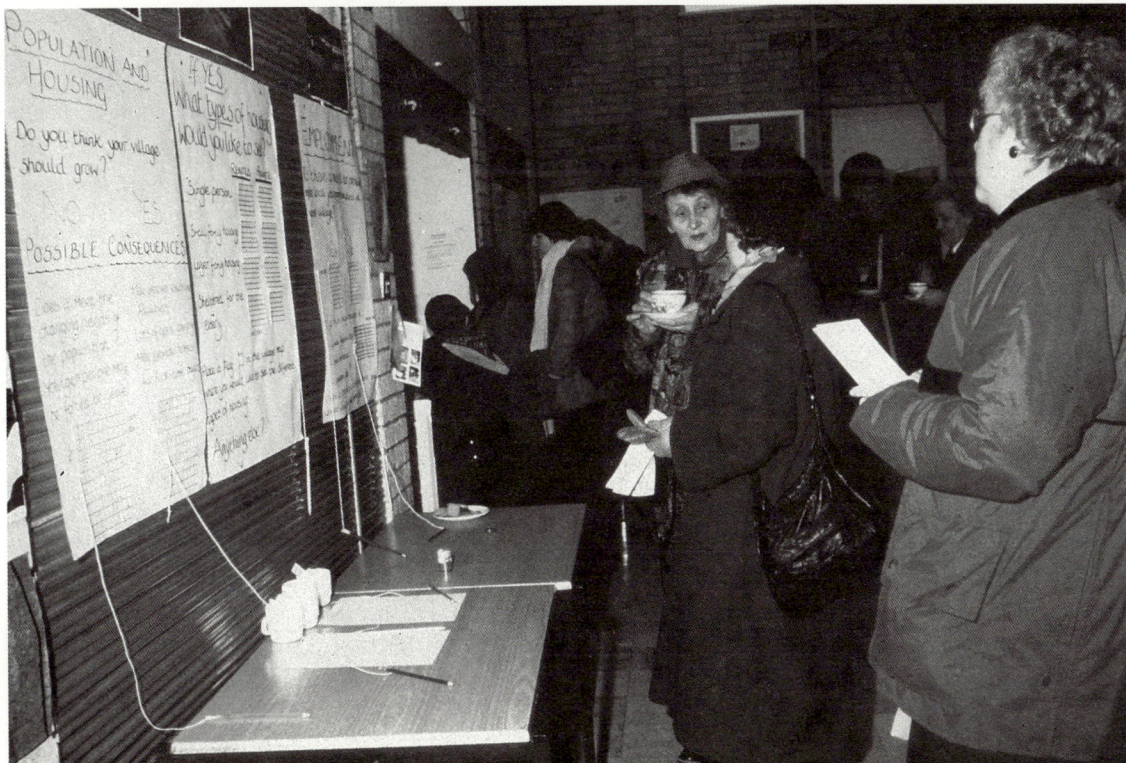

Local Plan meeting at Gilwern. Photo: Brecon Beacons National Park Authority

Appendix 1

Biodiversity Action Plan: priority species in National Parks, the New Forest and South Downs

Key
B Broads; BB Brecon Beacons; D Dartmoor; E Exmoor; NF New Forest; LD Lake District; NYM North York Moors; P Peak District; PC Pembrokeshire Coast; S Snowdonia; SD South Downs; Y Yorkshire Dales

Note: NPs is used if the species occurs in two or more of the National Parks (ie the original ten plus the Broads)

The two lowland areas worthy of National Park status are also included as NF for the New Forest and SD for the South Downs

If the species is only found in one National Park, the name of the Park is given.
Source: National Park Authority ecologists and the Sussex and Hanmpshire Wildlife Trusts, CNP survey 1996

Group	Scientific Name	Common name	Where found
Mammal	*Arvicola terrestris*	water vole	NPs, NF, SD
Mammal	*Lepus europaeus*	brown hare	NPs, NF, SD
Mammal	*Lutra lutra lutra*	European otter	NPs, NF, SD
Mammal	*Muscardinus avellanarius*	dormouse	NF, SD
Mammal	*Phocoena phocoena*	harbour porpoise	NPs
Mammal	*Pipistrellus pipistrellus*	pipistrelle bat	NPs
Mammal	*Rhinolophus ferrumequinum*	greater horseshoe bat	NPs
Mammal	*Sciurus vulgaris*	red squirrel	NPs
Bird	*Acropcephalus paludicola*	aquatic warbler	NPs
Bird	*Alauda arvensis*	skylark	NPs
Bird	*Botaurus stellaris*	bittern	NPs
Bird	*Burhinus oedicnemus*	stone curlew	SD
Bird	*Crex crex*	corncrake	NYM (during passage)
Bird	*Perdix perdix*	grey partridge	NPs, NF, SD
Bird	*Turdus philomelos*	song thrush	NPs, NF, SD
Amphibian	*Bufo calamita*	natterjack toad	NPs
Amphibian	*Triturus cristatus*	great crested newt	NPs, NF, SD
Amphibian	*Lacerta agilis*	sand lizard	S
Fish	*Alosa alosa*	allis shad	BB
Fish	*Alosa fallax*	twaite shad	BB
Fish	*Coregonus albula*	vendace	LD
Ants	*Formica candica (transkaucasica)*	bog ant	NF
Ants	*Formica exsecta*	narrow headed ant	NF (possibly extinct)
Beetle	*Aphodius niger*	a scarab beetle	NF

Group	Scientific Name	Common Name	Where found
Beetle	*Lucanus servus*	stag beetle	E, NF
Beetle	*Tachys edmondsi*	a ground beetle	NF (possibly extinct)
Butterfly	*Argynnis adippe*	high brown fritillary	E, PC (possibly)
Butterfly	*Boloria euphrosyne*	pearl-bordered fritillary	NPs, NF, SD
Butterfly	*Eurodrya aurinia*	marsh fritillary	NPs
Butterfly	*Hesperia comma*	silver-spotted skipper	SD
Butterfly	*Lycaena dispar*	large copper	potential: B
Butterfly	*Mellicta athalia*	heath fritillary	E
Cricket/grasshopper	*Gryllotalpa gryllotalpa*	mole cricket	NF possibly
Crustacean	*Austropotamobius pallipes*	freshwater white-clawed crayfish	NPs,NF
Damsel/dragonfly	*Coenagrion mercuriale*	southern damselfly	PC, NF
Fly	*Asilus crabroniformis*	a robber fly	NPs, SD possibly extinct
Fly	*Chrystoxum octomaculatum*	a hoverfly	NF
Mollusc	*Anisus vorticulus*	a snail	B
Mollusc	*Margaritifera margaritifera*	a freshwater pearl mussel	NPs
Mollusc	*Myxas glutinosa*	glutinous snail	S possibly
Mollusc	*Pseudanodonta complanata*	a freshwater mussel	B
Mollusc	*Vertigo geyeri*	a snail	NYM
Mollusc	*Vertigo moulinsiana*	a snail	SD, B
Moth	*Coscinia cribraria bivittata*	speckled footman	SD
Moth	*Eustroma reticulata*	netted carpet	LD
Sea Anemone Group	*Nematostella vectensis*	starlet sea anemone	NF
Worm	*Hirudo medicinalis*	medicinal leech	NPs, NF
Fungus	*Battarraea phalloides*	a phalloid	E
Fungus	*Boletus satanas*	Devil's bolete	SD
Fungus	*Poronia punctata*	nail fungus	NF
Lichen	*Caloplaca luteoalba*	orange-fruited elm lichen	NF possibly extinct
Lichen	*Collema dichotomum*	river jelly lichen	YD possibly
Lichen	*Pseudocyphellaria norvegica*	a lichen	S
Lichen	*Schismatomma graphidioides*	a lichen	E
Liverwort	*Petalophyllum ralfsii*	petalwort	NPs
Moss	*Hamatocaulis (Drepanocladus) vernicosusslender*	slender green feather-moss	S, NF
Moss	*Thamnobryum angustifolium*	Derbyshire feather moss	P PC
Vascular plant	*Alisma graminea*	ribbon-leaved water plantain	

Group	Scientific Name	Common Name	Where found
Vascular plant	*Cyripedium calceolus*	Lady's slipper orchid	YD
Vascular plant	*Euphrasia cambrica*	an eyebright	S
Vascular plant	*Euphrasia heslop-harrionii*	an eyebright	NPs
Vascular plant	*Euphrasia rivularis*	an eyebright	S
Vascular plant	*Euphrasia vigursii*	an eyebright	NPs
Vascular plant	*Gentianella anglica*	early gentian	NF, SD
Vascular plant	*Liparis loeselii*	fen orchid	B
Vascular plant	*Luronium natans*	floating water-plantain	NPs
Vascular plant	*Najas flexilis*	slender naiad	LD
Vascular plant	*Najas marina*	holly-leaved naiad	B
Vascular plant	*Ranunculus tripartitus*	three-lobed water crowfoot	PC
Vascular plant	*Trichomanes speciosum*	Killarney fern	NPs

Appendix 2

National Park female economic characteristics

	female population age 16-59	% female population age 16-59						
		total employed	economically active					economically inactive
			Employees		self employed	on a government scheme	Unemployed	
			F/T	P/T				
Park								
BB	8886	62.91	32.95	21.08	8.87	0.44	3.30	33.80
N	1187	58.89	24.09	24.09	10.70	1.01	3.03	37.07
D	8915	61.77	26.97	23.67	11.14	0.61	3.08	34.54
E	3215	62.61	23.64	21.18	17.79	0.37	3.76	33.25
LD	12424	69.49	34.06	21.15	14.27	0.58	2.13	27.80
NYM	7438	58.75	23.93	23.04	11.78	0.78	2.37	38.10
P	12586	65.04	29.73	25.40	9.91	0.52	2.33	32.12
PC	6461	53.26	23.51	18.88	10.87	1.19	4.83	40.72
S	7655	57.82	28.07	19.15	10.59	0.86	4.51	36.81
YD	5413	66.84	28.25	25.44	13.15	0.65	1.74	30.78
All Parks	74140	61.74	27.52	22.31	11.91	0.70	3.11	34.50
All RDAs	857292	60.22	29.61	23.58	7.04	0.91	3.75	35.12
Mid Wales	91303	59.75	30.50	20.17	9.08	0.98	3.42	35.83
GB	16196875	62.10	36.20	21.90	4.00	0.80	4.70	32.40

Compiled from 1991 Census of Population. Crown Copyright

Key: BB Brecon Beacons; N Northumberland; D Dartmoor; E Exmoor; LD Lake District; NYM North York Moor
P Peak; PC Pembrokshire Coast; S Snowdonia; YD Yorkshire Dales; RDA Rural Development Area

Glossary

Sustainable Development

Defined by the Brundtland Commission (1987) as "to meet the needs of present generations without compromising the ability of future generations to meet their own needs". The definition of needs is crucial and open to much interpretation, depending on perspectives. A big turning point as it introduced the idea of the environment into theories about economic development.

The Government sees it as the combination of achieving economic development to secure a higher standard of living now and for future generations whilst protecting and enhancing the environment.

Sustainability

What most environmental organisations would rather have than sustainable development as defined by the Government, which still implies the idea of growth. Sustainability is when policies are environment-led and growth is not an objective. It implies limits on activity, development and change.

Environmental sustainability

What this project is all about! It means sustaining the health of the environment now and for the future as a primary policy objective, for the sustenance of human life as well for the environment *per se*. Removes any confusion about sustainable development being about sustaining economic development at any environmental cost, which is how some rather mischievously interpret the idea.

Capital stock

Regarding the Earth's resources as capital from which income is derived rather than as an asset to be drawn down.

Critical loads

Part of the approach which implies that we can decide where the environmental limits to growth lie. A critical load is measurable – for instance, natural buffering systems mean that a soil can neutralise a certain amount of acid before becoming acidic itself.

Environmental capacity

Also part of deciding where environmental limits lie but more subjective and value-based. It implies that limits can be set beyond which irreversible environmental damage is caused.

Critics say this is an absolutist approach to human ecology as it suggests that "objective, immutable, unchallengeable, environmental criteria" exist (Grigson, Barton *cit.* 1995). Its main value may be in influencing policy makers: "it fixes in the minds of decision-makers, and especially politicians, that there are ultimately limits to the ability of environmental resources to accept demands upon them without irreversible or otherwise unacceptable loss or damage" (Coupe 1996)

Natural capital

All the natural things we value – but what is natural and how do we value it? Fraught with difficulties because of the implied need to apply economic valuation to elements for which financial valuation is probably impossible.

Critical natural assets/capital

The components of natural capital that we cannot afford to damage – vitally important and irreplaceable, where any loss or damage would be extremely serious. So these assets must be protected at all costs. CNP has long argued that National Parks are critical natural capital.

Biodiversity

The diversity of living things – important in its own right and we depend on it for our survival. The UK Action Plan for Biodiversity identifies key species and habitats and sets targets for them.

References

Baker Associates and Countrywise. 1995. Sustainability Appraisal of the Plans, Policies and Programmes of the Yorkshire Dales National Park Authority. Final report to the Countryside Commission and the Yorkshire Dales National Park Authority. Baker Associates, Bristol, and Countrywise, Hexham.

Bennett G. 1991. Towards a European Ecological Network. Institute for European Environmental Policy, Arnhem.

Biodiversity UK Steering Group. 1995. Meeting the Rio Challenge and Action Plans (2 Volumes). HMSO London.

Birkett N. 1945. National Parks and the Countryside. Standing Committee on National Parks, London.

Bridgewater P. 1996. Protected area management in the face of climate change. Parks, Vol. 6, No. 2. IUCN, Gland.

Cornish V. 1930. National Parks and the Heritage of Scenery. Sifton Praed, London.

Countryside Commission. 1986. The report of the Common Land Forum. CCP 215, Cheltenham.

Countryside Commission. 1991. Landscape Change in the National Parks. Countryside Commission, Cheltenham, CCP 359

Countryside Commission 1992. Trends in transport and the countryside. CCP 382.

Countryside Commission, Department of National Heritage, Rural Development Commission, English Tourist Board. 1995. Sustainable Rural Tourism – Opportunities for Local Action. Countryside Commission, Cheltenham.

Countryside Commission. 1995. Climate Change, Acidification and Ozone: Potential Impacts on the English Countryside. Countryside Commission CCP 458, Chelthenham

Countryside Commission. 1996. Corporate Plan (1996/97 – 1999/2000). Countryside Commission CCP 498. Cheltenham

Countryside Commission. 1996a. Visitors to National Parks. Countryside Commission CCP 503, Cheltenham.

Countryside Council for Wales. 1994. A policy framework for the coastal and marine zone of Wales. CCW Bangor.

Countryside Council for Wales. 1995. Overgrazing in Wales. CCW, Bangor.

Coupe M. 1996. Applying the Principles of Sustainability. Paper to the National Parks Workshop. English Heritage, London.

Council for the Preservation of Rural England, Sheffield and Peak District Committee. 1932. The Threat to the Peak. CPRE, Sheffield.

Countryside Council for Wales. 1996. Socio-economic Assessment of Tir Cymen, research report by ADAS for CCW. CCW, Bangor.

Countryside Council for Wales. 1996a. Transport and rural Wales. CCW, Bangor.

CPRE/WWF. 1996. Growing Greener – Sustainable Agriculture in the UK. CPRE, London, and WWF, Godalming.

Cynefin Environmental Consultants Ltd. 1996. Gwynedd's Coastal Zone and Marine Environment.

Department of the Environment. 1993. Third Report of the United Kingdom Photochemical Oxidants Review Group. HMSO.

Department of the Environment. 1994. Minerals Planning Guidance: Guidelines for Aggregates Provision in England. HMSO.

Department of the Environment/MAFF. 1995. Rural England, a nation committed to a living countryside. HMSO, London.

Department of the Environment. 1996. Indicators of Sustainable Development for the United Kingdom. HMSO, London

Department of the Environment. 1996a. Minerals Planning Guidance: general considerations and the development plan system. HMSO.

Department of the Environment and Welsh Office. 1992. Fit for the Future: A Statement by the Government on policies for the National Parks. Department of the Environment, London.

Dower J. 1945. National Parks in England and Wales. HMSO.

Dulas 1996. Energy Conservation in Snowdonia National Park, promoting its practical implementation. DULAS Ltd., Machynlleth

Dyrynda P.E.J. 1996. An appraisal of the early impacts of the Sea Empress oil spill on shore life in south-west Wales. University of Wales, Swansea.

Edwards, R. Chairman. 1991. Fit for the Future, report of the National Parks Review Panel. Countryside Commission CCP 334, Cheltenham.

Farmer, A.M., Bates J.W., Bell J.N.B. 1991. Comparisons of three woodland sites in NW Britain differing in richness of the epiphytic *Lobarion pulmonariae* community and levels of wet acidic deposition. Holarctic Ecology, 14: 85-91.

Friends of the Lake District. 1996. Water Conservation and Supply – memorandum of the Friends of the Lake District prepared for the House of Commons Environment Committee Inquiry. FLD, Kendal

Federation of Nature and National Parks of Europe. 1993. Loving them to Death? Sustainable tourism in Europe's Nature and National Parks. Grafenau, Germany.

Friends of the Earth. 1995. Losing Interest: a survey of threats to Sites of Special Scientific Interest in England and Wales. Friends of the Earth Trust Ltd., London.

Green Balance. 1993. Natural Assets: mineral working in National Parks. CNP, London.

Hamilton L.S. 1996. The Role of Protected Areas in Sustainable Mountain Development in PARKS, Vol. 6, No. 1, February 1996. IUCN, Gland.

Haworth E.Y. and Lishman J.P. 1991. Recent changes to upland tarns in the English Lake District. Hydrobiologia 214: 181 – 186.

Hobhouse A. 1947. Report of the National Parks Committee.

House of Commons Select Committee on the Environment. 1995. Report on the Environmental Impact of Leisure Activities. VOLS I-III. HMSO.

House of Lords Select Committee on Sustainable Development. 1995. Volume 1 – Report. HMSO.

Holve H. 1996. The Broads Natural Area Profile. English Nature/Broads Authority, Norwich

INDITE. 1994. Impacts of Nitrogen in Terrestrial Ecosystems. Department of the Environment, London.

IUCN. 1994. Parks for Life: Action for Protected Areas in Europe. IUCN, Gland, Switzerland.

IUCN/FAO/Icalpe 1996. European Inter-governmental Consultation 1996 on Sustainable Mountain Development. Towards Sustainable Mountain Development in Europe. IUCN, Gland, Switzerland.

Joint Nature Conservation Committee. 1996. The relative contribution of different sulphur point sources to acidification on SSSIs in Britain. Report No. 260. JNCC.

Local Government Management Board. 1995. Indicators for Local Agenda 21 – A Summary. LGMB, Luton, Beds.

Mabey R. 1996. Bold Vision Needed on Minerals Mining in Countryside March/April 1996 No. 78. Countryside Commission. Cheltenham.

MacEwen A. and M. MacEwen. 1987. Greenprints for the Countryside: the Story of Britain's National Parks. Allen and Unwin, London.

Meadows, D.H., D.L. Meadows and J. Randers. 1992. Beyond the Limits: Global Collapse or a Sustainable Future. Earthscan, London.

Mountain Agenda-UNCED initiating group. 1992. An Appeal for the Mountains. University of Berne.

North Yorkshire and Cleveland Heritage Coast Steering Group. 1995. Management Plan Second Review.

Oxford Centre for Tourism and Leisure Studies. 1996. Impact of Car Usage Study 1994-95. RAC Foundation for Motoring and the Environment.

Peak Park Joint Planning Board. 1990. Two Villages, Two Valleys: the Peak District Integrated Rural Development Project 1981 – 88. Peak National Park, Bakewell.

Peak National Park. 1995. 1991 Census – report for the Peak National Park. Peak Park, Bakewell.

Pearce D. (ed). 1993. Blueprint 3: Measuring Sustainable Development. Earthscan, London.

Royal Commission on Environmental Pollution. 1994. Transport and the Environment. HMSO.

Royal Commission on Environmental Pollution. 1996. Nineteenth Report. Sustainable Use of Soil. HMSO.

Smith P. 1975. The Politics of Physical Resources. Penguin, London.

Speakman C. 1992. Paper on Cultural Heritage and National Parks prepared for the Council for National Parks.

Speakman C. 1996. Paper on Environmentally Sensitive Tourism for the Society of National Park Staffs conference.

Symonds H.H. 1936. Afforestation in the Lakes. Dent, London.

Tourism and Recreation Research Unit. 1981. The Economy of Rural Communities in the National Parks of England and Wales. TRRU, University of Edinburgh.

United Kingdom Climate Change Impacts Review Group 1996. Review of the Potential Effects of Climate Change in the United Kingdom. HMSO, London

UK Government. 1990. This Common Inheritance. HMSO, London

UK Government. 1994. Sustainable Development, the UK Strategy. 1994. HMSO, London.

UK Government. 1994a. Biodiversity: the UK Action Plan. HMSO.

United Kingdom Report to the Commission of Sustainable Development. 1995. Department of the Environment, London.

United Nations Conference on Environment and Development. 1992. Earth Summit `92. Regency Press, London.

Whitehead PG et al 1996. Acidification in Three Lake District Tarns: Historical long term trends and modelled future behaviour under changing sulphate and nitrate deposition. Unpublished.

World Commission on Environment and Development. 1987. Brundtland Report. Oxford University Press.

Windermere in the Lake District National Park. Photo: Ian Brodie

"The value of protected areas to humanity has never been greater, but they have never been under greater pressure. If these areas are to succeed in making their contribution to sustainable development, they must adapt to these changes". IUCN, Parks for Life (1994).